THE GROUP DEPTH INTERVIEW

Principles and Practice

ALFRED E. GOLDMAN
SUSAN SCHWARTZ MCDONALD

National Analysts
Division of Booz, Allen & Hamilton Inc.

PH/ Series in Marketing / AMERICAN MARKETING ASSOCIATION

PRENTICE-HALL, INC., *Englewood Cliffs, New Jersey 07632*

Library of Congress Cataloging-in-Publication Data

Goldman, Alfred E.
  The group depth interview.

  Includes index.
  1. Interviewing in marketing research.
I. McDonald, Susan Schwartz. II. Title.
HF5415.2.G56 1987   658.8′3′028   86-22571
ISBN· 0-13-365396-X
ISBN   0-13-365404-4 (pbk.)

Editorial/production supervision and
  interior design: Marcia Rulfs
Cover Design: Ben Santora
Manufacturing buyer: Ed O'Dougherty

Printed in the United States of America

10 9 8 7 6 5 4 3 2 1

ISBN   0-13-365396-X   01

ISBN   0-13-365404-4   01   PBK

Prentice-Hall International (UK) Limited, *London*
Prentice-Hall of Australia Pty. Limited, *Sydney*
Prentice-Hall Canada Inc., *Toronto*
Prentice-Hall Hispanoamericana, S.A., *Mexico*
Prentice-Hall of India Private Limited, *New Delhi*
Prentice-Hall of Japan, Inc., *Tokyo*
Prentice-Hall of Southeast Asia Pte. Ltd., *Singapore*
Editora Prentice-Hall do Brasil, Ltda., *Rio de Janeiro*

Contents

Foreword

My first understanding of the potential of "the group depth interview" in marketing research came from Alfred E. Goldman's article by that title in the July 1962 issue of the *Journal of Marketing*. I learned even more when, with a client, I observed a complex group discussion moderated by Al Goldman. In 1984, I represented the American Marketing Association in a joint effort with Prentice-Hall to identify a series of books-that-need-to-be-written. Working with the marketing editor for Prentice-Hall, Elizabeth Classon, a key need was identified for a solid book on qualitative research, and more particularly, the group depth interview. Because of his role in the introduction and development of this approach to research in marketing, Al Goldman was our natural choice. We are all pleased that he was able to secure the assistance of his colleague, Dr. Susan Schwartz McDonald, and bring this book to fruition.

Qualitative research has achieved growing respect, use, and support over the last couple of decades. From a tenuous beginning in the 1950s, a real growth began in the 1960s and continues through the 1980s. In spite of this, one can examine the library of marketing research texts and fail to recognize the key role played by qualitative methods in the marketing discipline. One cannot, however, spend a week in the world of marketing research without realizing that qualitative group studies are as common as surveys. This book will help to redress this imbalance.

The reader will find in this book both theory and practice. The real emphasis is on the practical use of group interview methodologies. While the abundant psychological theory on which the methods are based is not discussed extensively, the reader is aware throughout of the depth of understanding that informs the text. One is aware that Drs. Goldman and McDonald have brought to this book their strong academic backgrounds, just as they bring them to their work with groups, and to their training and development of others in this art/science.

The book contains a comprehensive treatment of the subject. The reader will come away understanding when to use the group depth interview methods—as well as when not to use them. The development and use of proper facilities for this very special research setting are fully discussed.

The bulk of the book deals with how to carry out the research. The design of the study, the details of conducting the study, the analysis of the data, and the writing of the report are all covered thoroughly. A crucial part of actually conducting group depth interviews is the moderator's skill in eliciting information. Treatment of the "probing" skills is well illustrated with verbatim quotations from actual groups. Indeed, these "verbatims" are included throughout the book. They add realism and drive home the points with clarity.

There are at least three groups who should read this book. The first includes group moderators—who will learn much about their craft—and those who aspire to be moderators. Indeed, this would be an ideal textbook in courses for moderators-in-training. The second group is made up of marketing research generalists who often have to help fit the right method to the problem at hand, as well as to understand how qualitative research can contribute to a larger research program often involving quantitative methods as well.

The third group consists of product and marketing managers who are the "customers," or the users of research results. While they may not wish to understand fully how to do the research, this book will make them better users of these important methodologies. As the authors correctly point out, it takes both capable researchers and capable users to make the method work.

A final group that should find the book helpful is made up of my fellow marketing educators. Not only would the book broaden our understanding of a research tool of increasing usefulness, it could serve as a supplemental text in marketing research courses.

—Peter D. Bennett
The Pennsylvania State University

Acknowledgments

Perhaps the most enjoyable task for an author is to write the preface. Not only does it signal completion of the manuscript, but it offers the opportunity to express appreciation to those who have contributed in some way to what we have written.

We express our gratitude to our firm, Booz, Allen & Hamilton, for consistent encouragement of professional excellence. Special thanks go to Dr. Marshall Greenberg, President of the National Analysts Division and close colleague and friend to us both, for maintaining the kind of professional and intellectual environment in which the effort required to write this book was warmly supported. We cannot mention by name all the many other colleagues in the firm and elsewhere whose suggestions and encouragement contributed to our efforts.

Our appreciation is also due to those patient and persistent helpers, Josephine Rendech, Anita Moorer, and Catherine Berry, who converted what was, at times, barely legible script into typed text, and who persevered through many rounds of corrections and additions.

We also wish to convey our thanks to Drs. Herbert Abelson and Peter Bennett for their thorough and insightful reviews of our manuscript and their many helpful suggestions, most of which are reflected in the final product.

Finally, we dedicate this book to our spouses, Adele Goldman and Graham McDonald, and to our children, Elizabeth, Nora, and Geoffrey McDonald and Julie and Marshall Goldman. They have often had to do without us while we crisscrossed the nation conducting groups and conferring with clients. While the effort of plying this craft is ours, our families have also contributed to whatever success we have enjoyed, with their patient acceptance of our frequent absences and their cheering encouragement of our professional labors.

In addition, Julius and Louise Judith Schwartz also deserve special mention for having conveyed to their daughter, Susan, that writing books was one of the proudest and most distinguished endeavors a person could undertake, and for inspiring completion throughout the long creative process by repeatedly asking, "So when are you two going to finish?"

Alfred E. Goldman
Susan Schwartz McDonald

The Origin of the Group Interview

Chapter 1

INTRODUCTION

Qualitative research, and especially the procedure known as the group depth interview (or "focus group") is one of the most important, the most widely used, and arguably, the most psychologically valid tool of market research. The number of group interview projects commissioned each year far exceeds the number of surveys, and group interviews are now used for a wide range of purposes beyond traditional marketing applications, including media checks for political candidates, institutional self-appraisals, and mock trials to anticipate jury deliberations. Nevertheless, while there are many handbooks and how-to manuals of survey research in print, to date few texts have been written to guide marketing professionals in the techniques and uses of group depth interviews.

The omission has a great deal to do with the nature of qualitative methods. As with any blend of art and science, the mix of stage management and research technique in group interviews defies easy instruction. In sharp contrast with a statistical manipulation or a head count, no qualitative interview can be precisely replicated; each one will always be unique.

This is not to suggest that qualitative research is without its rules and protocols. Mastery of group moderating techniques requires extensive training, scrupulous attention to detail, and a recognition that even skilled application of the rules cannot ensure predictable outcomes. It may be helpful to think of the group interview as an improvised performance, not unlike courtroom procedure. For the trial attorney, there are goals and directions and a set of performance rules, but no script. The emphasis in both cases is on revelation and disclosure, although lawyers may deliberately skirt the truth in pursuit of adversarial advantage. In both cases, however, the validity of the proceedings lies in the process as well as the outcome. Process and outcome are, in fact, inextricably linked.

There are, of course, some important differences: the trial attorney is a partisan while the moderator is, or should be, an agent of strict neutrality. The success of a group interview depends largely on the skill of the moderator in guiding participants without dominating or subverting them. Both professionals, however, play the combined role of performer, artistic director, and stage manager in an unscripted proceeding whose goal is disclosure. The similarities and the challenges are striking.

We undertook the writing of this book because of our conviction that the ability to conduct group depth interviews *can* be communicated. The technique has a structure and principles that can be taught to others, although we acknowledge that it is not possible to make a talented moderator out of everyone, just as it is not possible to develop in everyone a flair for theatrical performance or an aptitude for statistics.

Our goal in writing this book is twofold. First, we wish to guide those who intend to become practitioners in the techniques of qualitative interviewing, particularly group interviewing. Second, we wish to help people who use qualitative research do so in a knowledgeable and effective way. Our goal is to cultivate both skilled players and knowledgeable, discriminating audiences, since ultimately the practice of valid, useful qualitative research depends on the existence of both.

THE GENESIS AND GROWTH OF THE GROUP DEPTH INTERVIEW

The group depth interview traces its roots to the diverse methods of the behavioral scientist and the psychotherapist. "Focus groups," the popular (though ungrammatical) term that most often identifies the technique, derives initially from the method of interviewing individual respondents developed by Robert K. Merton, the well-known sociologist. It was described in a manual, co-authored with Patricia L. Kendall, entitled "The Focussed Interview" in March of 1944 and published two years later in the *American Journal of Sociology.*[1]

[1]Robert K. Merton and Patricia L. Kendall, "The Focussed Interview" *American Journal of Sociology* LI, no. 6 (May 1946): 541–57.

The distinguishing characteristic of the focused interview is that interviewees have been exposed to concrete situations, the 'objective' character of which is known to, and has been previously analyzed by, the interviewer. The interviewees have seen a film; heard a radio program; read a pamphlet, magazine or advertisement; participated in a psychological experiment. In other words, the interview focusses on one experience of the respondent—exposure to a given stimulus situation, a situation which the interviewer has subjected to a 'content analysis' which in turn has formed the basis of an 'interview guide.'

The principal contribution of Merton and Kendall to the development of group depth interviewing is the guidance they provide for conducting interviews with a circumscribed focus. Stanley Payne, in his very useful book *The Art of Asking Questions*,[2] elaborates the general principles of interpersonal inquiry that are equally helpful in conducting interviews singly or in groups.[3]

The legacy of psychologists and psychiatrists in the development of this technique was their commitment to the pursuit of unconscious motivation and their application of probing techniques designed to expose those motives without altering them. Carl Rogers' nondirective technique has been of special value.[4]

Experience in managing the interpersonal exchange in group psychotherapy also contributed much to the development of the group interview in market research. Indeed, some of the earliest practitioners of the group interview had been group psychotherapists in hospital and clinic settings.[5]

From this rich stew of sociopsychological and psychotherapeutic traditions and techniques emerged the group depth interview and its marketing applications. Interviews conducted in a group setting were described in the research literature as early as the 1940s [6,7] but earliest attempts to apply the method to advertising and marketing problems can be traced to 1949 and the early 1950s. Like many inventions, this one appears to have

---

[2]S.L. Payne, *The Art of Asking Questions* (Princeton, NJ: Princeton University Press, 1951).

[3]No attempt will be made here to summarize the vast literature on interviewing techniques or unconscious motivation. For those who wish to explore those subjects in greater depth see: W.V. Bingham and B.U. Moore, *How to Interview*, (New York: House of Harper, 1941); H. Sherman and S. Presser, *Questions and Answers in Attitude Surveys* (New York: Academic Press, Inc., 1981).

[4]C.R. Rogers, *Counseling and Psychotherapy*, (New York; Houghton Mifflin Company, 1941).

[5]H.H. Lerner and H.C. Kelmen, "*Group Methods in Psychotherapy, Social Work, and Adult Education,*" *Journal of Social Issues* 8, No. 2 (1952) pp. 1–88.

[6]Vivian Edmiston, "*The Group Interview,*" *Journal of Educational Research* 37, (April 1944) pp. 593–601.

[7]Mark Abrams, "*Possibilities and Problems of Group Interviewing,*" *Public Opinion Quarterly* 13, (Fall 1949) pp. 502–506.

surfaced spontaneously in several different places so that it is difficult to credit any one individual with true patrimony.

The earliest group interview that could be identified as such from discussions with early pioneers in qualitative research, was conducted in 1949 by Ted Nowak, then with Alderson and Sessions in Philadelphia.[8] The study was conducted for Pablum as the prelude to a survey. Thus, infant food was the first beneficiary of the nascent technique. Shortly thereafter Nowak had a second opportunity to apply group interviewing in a study of the acceptability of a low sudsing detergent by housewives. Since the client's budget did not permit a large in-home survey, Nowak decided to distribute samples of the new product to homemakers and then invite them into his office for a group interview.

In 1950 Dr. Perham C. Nahl, an economist then on the staff of Needham, Louis and Brorby, Inc., interviewed a group of black consumers to gain insight into their reaction to ads created by the agency. He termed the method the "snowball interview." In an article published in 1951, Dr. Nahl explained the origin of the term. "We call it the snowball interview because it gets a group into a frame of mind where their comments build up cumulatively to a total sum of information greater than that obtained in the door-to-door type interview."[9]

The principal benefits of the method, according to Nahl were the greater depth and breadth of information generated at lower cost than individual depth interviews, and the opportunity for researchers to learn the language of the buyer.

Dr. George Horsely Smith, a psychologist then with the Grey Advertising Agency, conducted a group interview in 1951 that he regarded as an experiment. The client, a marketer of whiskey, was interested in learning more about the process and determinants of purchase. Because the results were required in a few days, Smith sought a methodological alternative to the traditional in-home survey. Struck by the broader applicability of group interviewing, Smith presented his ideas later in 1951 in an address entitled "Interviewing in Groups."[10] Early success with the method prompted Smith to install group interviewing as a part of his marketing research armamentarium. Group interviews were then used principally to develop new business, to evaluate advertising strategy, and to evaluate its implementation in copy.

Sidney First, a researcher with Batten, Barton, Durstine & Osborn,

---

[8]An exhaustive list of all those who used the group interview early in its development exceed the purview of this brief introduction to the history of group interviewing.

[9]Perham C. Nahl, *The Snowball Interview - New Tool for Market Research, Printers Ink,* March 23, 1951.

[10]Later published in: George H. Smith, *Motivation Research in Advertising and Marketing* (Westport, Conn: Greewood Press, 1954).

Inc., began using group interviews in 1953. First, whose initial groups were held to pretest questionnaires, was at that time unaware of Nahl and Smith's early efforts. He soon recognized the potential of group interviews for evaluating new product concepts, and one of the earliest studies conducted by First was an assignment on behalf of the duPont company to explore reaction to the concept of shaving cream in an aerosol can.

Another advertising agency that contributed to the development of the group interview was Tatham Laird in Chicago, for whom Mimi Lieber conducted her first group interview in 1955. Her early group interviews focused upon the American housewife and the changing role of women in the 1950s. She may have provided subsequent legions of moderators with a prototype and role model for the free-lance moderator when she started her own consulting practice in 1959. Qualitative research consulting has since evolved into a sizeable cottage industry, as reflected in the growing membership of the Qualitative Research Consultants Association.

The mid and late 1950s saw increasing experimentation with group interviewing by several practitioners in marketing research agencies. In 1956, Mr. Benjamin Gedalecia, a political scientist who headed the research department at Batten, Barton, Durstine & Osborne, Inc., commissioned a study of a prospective campaign for B. F. Goodrich. He contracted with Dr. Joseph Smith, a clinical psychologist who had recently established a research agency (Oxtoby-Smith), to conduct the study using the group method. The utility of the results led Gedalecia to hire Bayard Badenhausen as a full-time staff psychologist. Badenhausen's principal efforts were directed to conducting research using the group technique. Later, in 1957, Dr. Thomas Coffin, marketing research director of NBC, asked Oxtoby-Smith to evaluate pilot programs of television series using group interviewing techniques. Frank Kennedy moderated the groups. Both Coffin and Kennedy had been trained in clinical psychology.

In 1957, Dr. Herbert Abelson, a psychologist then with Opinion Research Corporation, began exploring the use of group interviews after having discovered their usefulness quite by accident. Several respondents who had been recruited for individual interviews showed up at the same time, since some were late and others early. Rather than have them wait for him to complete the interviews in sequence, he decided to interview them collectively. The additional information yielded by the interaction among the respondents prompted his further development of the technique.

In Philadelphia, also in 1957, Dr. Alfred E. Goldman of National Analysts applied his prior experience as a group psychotherapist to the development of the group depth interview. He was especially interested in developing the method for investigating the motivational substructure of the behavior of executives and professionals, particularly physicians.

In Chicago, among the earliest to use group interviews in marketing research agencies (1959) were Drs. Irving White and Saul Ben-Zeev of

Creative Research Associates. At the same time, the pioneering qualitative research of Burleigh Gardner of Social Research, Inc., demonstrated the usefulness of the intensive (often up to several hours) individual interviews and facilitated the emergence of group interviewing.

By 1960 the group interview had come to be widely acknowledged as a legitimate research procedure, and the number of group interview studies commissioned grew exponentially. Even as late as the early 1960s, most groups were conducted in a recruiter's or a participant's living room, if not in a hotel room. Observers usually sat in the same room somewhere off to the side where they would be less obtrusive.

Today, almost all group interviews are conducted in facilities specially designed for that function. Virtually all provide a one-way mirror; some permit observation by means of closed-circuit television. Group interviewing can be conducted in facilities in every major city and many smaller ones in the United States and in a number of other countries around the world. The remarkable growth of group interviewing is suggested by the increase in rooms that permit observation of groups by one-way mirror or CCTV. In the United States alone, there are reported to be over 700 group interviewing facilities.[11]

There exists no reliable estimate of the total dollars invested in group interviews by marketing research agencies, advertising agencies, advertisers, manufacturers and public relations companies. A gross estimate, however, may be derived by considering the number of group rooms, the average number of groups conducted in each room per year, and an informed guess regarding the average total cost per group (including recruiting, incentives, moderating, analysis and report). Using this admittedly imprecise formula, it appears that the dollar volume spent on group interview studies conducted for advertising and market research in 1985 was between $283 and $378 million.[12] This amount exceeds the total gross national product of many small nations.[13]

---

[11]*The National Directory of Focus Group Discussion Facilities and Moderators* (Riverside, CT: 1984).

[12]The estimate is based on the 740 group interview facilities identified in the National Directory of Focus Group Discussion facilities and Moderators, Riverside, CT 1984. Of those reported we assume that perhaps 700 are actively using their facilities for group interviews. If each facility has an average of 1.5 group rooms this would yield 1,050 group rooms in the United States in field services, full service research agencies and advertising agencies. The estimate of 1.5 group rooms per facility seems conservative since an informal poll of 96 members of the Marketing Research Association in the Spring of 1986 suggests an average of 2.7 rooms per facility.

Multiplying the number of group rooms by an average of 12 groups conducted per room (M.R.A. survey) in an average month (12,600) for 11 months (to account for the weeks in which few groups are conducted due to holidays) yields 138,600 groups per year. If each group costs an average of $2,250 then the total expenditure for group interviews in the U.S. is approximately $312 million dollars.

[13]United States State Department, *Background Notes*, 1984.

The Definition
of Group Interviews

Chapter 2

THE DIFFERENCE BETWEEN QUALITATIVE AND
QUANTITATIVE RESEARCH

We have been discussing the evolution of group interviews and qualitative research generally, but have neglected to define them, partly because qualitative research seems to be most easily defined in terms of what it is *not*. Unlike quantitative research, which concerns itself with counting things to arrive at statistically projectable data, qualitative research addresses the nature or structure of attitudes and motivations rather than their frequency and distribution. Whether one chooses to conduct group or individual interviews, the underlying goal of qualitative investigations is always the same: to explore in depth the feelings and beliefs people hold, and to learn how these feelings shape overt behavior.

There are two basic methods of qualitative research. The *group* depth interview, commonly called focus group, assembles eight to ten respondents in the presence of a trained moderator who guides a discussion lasting about two hours. A typical study consists of two to eight of these sessions.

The *individual* depth interview (or IDI) collects information serially in a one-on-one session that generally lasts about 45 minutes to an hour. From

5 to 50 such interviews (occasionally more) may be conducted in a single qualitative study, and they can be used along with or instead of group interviews. Such studies are less commonly commissioned than group projects, but we discuss their uses and limitations in the final chapter.

Both group and individual interviews are customarily tape recorded for later review and analysis. Depending on the setting, either type of interview may be observed through a one-way mirror. Analysis of the data addresses how people feel and why, rather than how many of them have expressed specific opinions or reported particular behaviors. As a result, when you have completed a qualitative study, you do not know how statistically representative of the universe your findings might actually be. For example, even if seven out of ten people interviewed in a qualitative setting express enthusiasm for a particular product or idea, it is entirely possible that in a broader survey of the market, seven in ten might actually reject that same product.

If the opportunity for statistical error is so great in qualitative research, why conduct it? The answer is that although qualitative research does not tell you how widely distributed an attitude or motivation might be, it does tell you—and in ways surveys cannot—from where those attitudes arise, how they are structured, and what broader significance they may have for consumer behavior. The rich qualitative insights that spring from close inspection of individuals can never be duplicated by large-scale surveys, which view the market from a more distant vantage point.

Before discussing in detail how to conduct qualitative research and groups in particular, we would like to review how they are different from surveys and the implications of those differences. In order to understand the distinction more fully, it is important to review the nature of "truth" and "error" as social science research tends to define them.

In marketing research, as in all of social science, we concern ourselves with two principal sources of error: *sampling error* and *measurement error*. The presence or absence of sampling error reflects the degree to which the people, events, or attitudes we have sampled for a study are truly representative of the universe from which they are drawn. Another term to describe that is "reliability." Operationally, reliability is a measure of the extent to which the results of a study can be replicated in successive measurement attempts. Reliability implies that if we were to conduct the same survey with another sample drawn from the same universe, the results would be essentially the same.

Statistical reliability reflects not only the manner in which we select respondents but also the way in which we actually sample their opinions. Thus, in order for data to be reliable, all respondents must be asked the same set of questions in the same way.

Measurement error is concerned not with the selection of the sample but with how successfully we have captured that which we seek to mea-

location and participate in a group of interview are different, not
m the general population, but also from people who participate in
. While group interview respondents are undoubtedly self-selected
: sense, we must not overlook the fact that participation in any
ı effort is voluntary.

:tual experience with both methodologies suggests to us that what-
ial or psychological basis it may have, a willingness to participate in a
ive research effort does not have clearcut or important implications
 research findings. (The frequency with which survey data tend to
 qualitative findings offers reassurance on that point.) Although one
always be aware that self-selection may distort any research metho-
 it is no more a limitation on groups than on any other method.

lestion structure and sequence One element of statistical reliability is
ımption that all respondents will be asked every question in pre-
ıe same way time after time. Systematic variations may be intro-
'or one reason or another, but they are always controlled and are
y devised to measure or offset the effects of those variations on the
 we plan to aggregate the responses of a large sample, and especially
xpect to perform statistical procedures on the data, every respon-
ould be asked the same question in the same words and in a consequence. This approach is characteristic of survey research but is
ınpatible with qualitative research, where each interview is unique
: flow and wording of questions will be spontaneous and variable.
:mise of qualitative research is that questions must vary in response
haracter and requirements of each individual or group exchange.
, successive rewording of questions to elicit more profound infor-
is a requirement of good moderating.

nitations on the Validity of a Quantitative Study

/ contrast, when we apply the criterion of validity, the importance
ique value of qualitative research become immediately apparent.
)en and flexible structure of qualitative research gives the inter-
greater latitude in the way questions are phrased or rephrased and,
 important, it leaves participants with the same degree of latitude
xibility in the way they respond. The fact that questions are being
y a research professional who can interpret responses and guide the
w in accordance with the requirements of the analysis ultimately
:s data of greater validity than structured interviews.

 addition, the presence of other respondents who question and
 with one another in a group interview also helps to elicit responses
: more candid and certainly more richly detailed than survey data.
sense, we say that qualitative findings, though certainly not subject

sure—in other words, the validity of our data. Ve
that developing valid measures of attitudes or bel
prime example are the intent-to-purchase scale
searchers attempt to predict new product interest (
have been devised to measure purchase intent
questions are structured, the resulting projections
ity. There are several reasons for that.

First, consumers may not choose to tell us
measurement scale we provide may not adequatel
ties of their feelings; and third, consumers themse
predict future behavior. Our careful attempts to
with clarity and sensitivity are all aimed at bridgin
surement techniques and actual feelings or beha\
data depends upon how successfully we are able t

All aspects of the study design including the s;
procedure, and the method of data collection sele
the statistical reliability and validity of the findin
however, we regard a survey, which asks a large
same questions in precisely the same way, as more
potentially less valid than a qualitative study, which
respondents similar questions in somewhat differe
sections explain why.

Limitations on the Reliability of a Qualitative Stı

Sample size The number of respondents custo
qualitative study falls far short of the number of ind
to survey for statistically projectable results. The sar
study may be as small as ten and is generally no l
uncommon for surveys to include as many as 1,000
sample sizes of several hundred are adequate for r

Sampling Procedure In a truly projectable su
screened and enlisted on a probability basis so tha
selection shape the structure of the sample, and th
respondent self-selection or interviewer convenier
contrast, respondents in a qualitative study are seldo
basis because statistical projectability is not the goal. (
ity govern the selection and number of responden
researchers often choose to overlook whole market se
age groups or user types) in order to better focus a q
Although qualitative research is not statisticall
pling limitations unique to groups are occasionall
particular exception to the premise that responden

to precise replication, are a more psychologically valid representation of how people think and feel than survey responses.

To illustrate that distinction, imagine a survey question which asked you which you preferred: apple pie or chocolate cake. Let us assume, furthermore, that you like them both a great deal but that the interview instructions require you to select one over the other. Note that however unfair this approach may seem, it is frequently used in marketing research precisely because it discourages people from sitting on the fence.

Quantification does not cope well with ambivalence or ambiguity. It assumes that while people often express feelings of neutrality, they generally have, and should be made to express, some subtle preference.

Let us suppose that having resisted the temptation to check off both answers or skip the question entirely, you grudgingly check apple pie. Here is how such a questioning sequence might go in a qualitative interview:

Q: Which do you prefer: apple pie or chocolate cake?
A: I don't know, I like them both.
Q: Well, if you had to give up one or the other, which would it be, do you think?
A: Actually, it depends. If we're talking about my mother's apple pie, then I prefer that to any chocolate cake. But if we're just talking about anyone's apple pie, then I don't know. It depends, I guess, on a bunch of things.
Q: On what other things does it depend?
A: Well, it depends on what I've had for dinner, for example. If I've had a heavy dinner, I think I'd probably go for the pie. And on Thanksgiving, it's pie for sure. That's a big tradition in my family. But, I don't know, after something light like fish, chocolate cake is great. That is, if it has frosting. I don't care for plain chocolate cake.

Notice that the simple answer, "apple pie," though not inaccurate, is a limited statement of fact whose chief virtue is that it can be tallied and replicated. It fails, however, to capture a wealth of information about the circumstances under which apple pie may be preferred and the limitations on that preference (for example, whose pie?) or the factors which shape it (such as tradition or preceding courses). If you are planning a dessert menu it would certainly help for you to know these contingencies, although a tally of preferences for apple pie versus chocolate cake would be very useful as well.

The subject matter, pie versus cake, may not seem initially to justify so lengthy an exchange, and yet important marketing decisions often reflect pedestrian preferences. Indeed, one quickly learns that no matter how simple or mundane the product, whether it be bathroom cleanser or pet food, the motivations which govern its use are as complex as those which drive more exotic or "important" behavior.

This hypothetical exchange makes a case for the validity of qualitative research. One might, however, legitimately question whether some other interviewer, less skilled or more directive, might have elicited essentially the same series of responses from the same respondent. In asking that question, we are raising issues of both validity and reliability. Ultimately, neither one has value or meaning without the other. Imagine, for example, the thermometer which is consistently wrong—that is to say, reliably inaccurate—or the thermometer which registers the correct temperature only some of the time.

It is certainly true that no two qualitative interviews will ever be precisely the same because they are improvisations rather than scripted performances. And it is also true that some interviewers will be more successful than others at eliciting complete and valid information, and that some analysts will be capable of more sensitive interpretations. Both the processes of eliciting data and interpreting it are more complex and more judgmental in qualitative research than in quantitative research because surveys structure and streamline data to facilitate counting. Qualitative research, on the other hand, makes uncensored use of whatever can be tapped. It relies not only on verbal expressions but also on a rich bank of gestures, facial expressions, even omissions—what *wasn't* said as well as what was.

Lest qualitative research appear too subjective and quixotic, however, it should be emphasized that (1) it is possible to instruct people in principles of qualitative investigation which increase its practical validity and reliability and (2) even survey methods, if improperly applied, can become as impressionistic and unsound as qualitative research in the wrong hands. There are no techniques so robust or resilient that they can withstand the misuse of a poorly-trained practitioner.

The Uses of Qualitative Research

Chapter 3

Qualitative research can be designed in either of two ways. It can be a self-contained study without a follow-up survey or an exploratory phase in a multiphase quantitative project. Occasionally, the normal sequence is reversed and qualitative research steps are scheduled *after* a survey to help explain or embellish quantitative results. By logic and custom, however, qualitative research normally precedes quantitative research because survey analysis implies a progressive tightening of focus and a validation or refinement of qualitative hypotheses.

These two applications—preliminary and independent studies—warrant separate discussion because although the same sorts of techniques are used in both, their goals and end products may be very different. Each type of study, therefore, has different liberties and limitations.

We have chosen to first discuss how qualitative research functions in the context of quantitative studies, or preliminary research, because there is probably little controversy or ambiguity about its value in that setting. Clients who are inclined to worry about the overuse or reliability of qualitative research tend to find reassurance in the fact that a survey is expected to follow. We then discuss the appropriate use of independent or free-standing qualitative research, and finally, we review some specialized applications that we believe are methodologically inappropriate or ill advised.

PRELIMINARY (PRESURVEY) RESEARCH

There are several related applications of preliminary or exploratory qualitative research. For a researcher who is unfamiliar with a particular market or for a veteran who has not had current exposure to it, exploratory research can make the difference between a sound survey design and a faulty one, between a sensitive questionnaire and a poor one. It has particular value in markets which are technical or complex such as medicine or telecommunications, but it can be extremely helpful even in more prosaic and better known product categories.

This is not meant to suggest that qualitative research should take the place of formal preparation, for example, of collecting and reviewing available secondary data. It can, however, provide insights that are less readily available or sometimes overlooked in secondary market data.

One case that comes to mind concerned a product targeted for use in trucks and brought to us for market testing by a prospective licensor. The appliance was designed to operate off truck lighters; only by talking to groups of professional drivers did we and our client discover that such lighters are not standard equipment in trucks. The client then went back to the drawing board rather than forward to more market research.

Preliminary group interview research can also confirm the marketing relevance of a research investigation. In one such instance, exploratory group interviews were conducted to evaluate public acceptance of the package design of a prescription product that would, in most cases, be kept in the medicine cabinet. One initial hypothesis questioned the value of such a study because it was assumed that no one other than the user, or members of the immediate family, would ever open someone else's medicine chest and see the package. However, group interviews revealed that women, especially younger ones, often do open the medicine cabinets of friends to satisfy curiosity about what drug products they use. The finding that "what's in a medicine chest is the best way to learn what somebody is like," indicated that assumptions about the privacy of the medicine cabinet are unwarranted and confirmed the relevance of further package testing.

Preliminary qualitative research is an especially important starting point for studies designed to explore unfamiliar markets or test and screen new product or concept evaluations. It may also illuminate reasons for disappointing share or penetration that would otherwise escape detection in an ordinary survey. It is not, however, generally required prior to market tracking studies or otherwise routine surveys of well-understood markets. The principal contributions it can make to a survey include:

Hypothesis Generation

One of the most important applications of qualitative research is its use in developing hypotheses for quantiative testing. Clients and researchers often generate creative hypotheses without a qualitative stimulus, but it is unwise to rely entirely on professional hunches, even when the product category is a familiar one. These examples illustrate the point.

A client was test marketing a household disinfectant with a considerably milder and less astringent odor than the current market leader. When repeat purchase fell below expectations, group interviews were conducted to identify possible reasons. What was discovered in the groups might not have been identified if the client had proceeded directly to a market survey. It turned out that in solving what was believed to be problem or deficiency of existing cleaners, the manufacturer had actually created a new and more serious one. By masking the astringent odor, the company had deprived consumers of something they evidently valued: sensory reassurance that the product was indeed working and a clear signal to others that the user was a conscientious homemaker.

In another instance, we conducted group interviews to educate ourselves about the purchase process surrounding painting equipment before attempting to determine what triggered or discouraged acquisition of a new tool. The groups suggested that women played a more important role than we had previously imagined in setting the process in motion but that they frequently deferred to men for "ratification" of final product selection. That hypothesis was tested and confirmed in a comprehensive survey.

Research Design

Although the survey is often designed in advance of qualitative research, the exploratory phase can help us to fine tune the survey methodology and may occasionally even persuade us to abandon it. For example, based on groups, we may decide that some market segments are too marginal in importance to justify any (or equal) representation in a survey, or that some traditionally overlooked segments should be given more serious attention. Women, for example, may or may not be a productive group to survey on home repair issues, while men may be of little use in a study of cooking appliances. We have, in some studies, opted to exclude primary care physicians from surveys about therapeutic areas in which they seem only to review prescriptions originated by specialists. The role they play in ratifying and perpetuating these drug decisions is often not well understood until groups are concluded.

We also find that in some markets, the way people typically characterize themselves is so vague or inaccurate that we may need special screening procedures to locate relevant survey respondents. Qualitative research experience, for example, has led us to conclude that virtually everyone considers themselves to be "health conscious". If we wish to survey prospective health food purchasers, we have to apply more stringent and more carefully worded operational criteria, and group interviews have helped us to devise those in the past.

One of the more helpful design applications is in planning market segmentation studies. Segmentation analysis describes a series of statistical procedures which classify respondents on the basis of attitude or motivation profiles rather than on the basis of some unidimensional attribute like usage frequency or brand preference. In planning segmentation studies, we are sometimes faced with a decision about whether to focus on people or on usage occasions. The decision depends almost entirely on whether we believe that the product motivations within a particular market are stable across usage occasions—that is to say, whether people react in much the same why for the same reasons time after time. Usage needs and motivations may actually vary across occasions in a way that discourages individuals from successfully generalizing about what they do.

An example of the former category would be a "personal trademark" item like cigarettes. People usually select the same brand every time for reasons that remain consistent across both purchase and smoking situations. By contrast, different needs may be operating each time a person selects a cold beverage. Occasions may be driven by thirst, by boredom, or social requirements, and the product or brand selected will often reflect those variable psychological requirements.

It is essential that we make a decision about what to segment—people or occasions—before designing a questionnaire. In many cases, the decision is a fairly easy one, but more often we find ourselves faced with a continuum rather than a clear dichotomy. Most product choices are governed by both situational variables and stable personal needs and traits. In markets where a reasonable argument can be made for both person- and occasion-based methodologies, qualitative research can guide the decision by uncovering the needs that shape product usage and selection.

Questionnaire Construction

Qualitative research supports questionnaire construction in a number of ways, but one of the most basic services it performs is to acquaint us with the terms and phrases consumers use in talking about products and services. It is common for marketers to use terminology which is unfamiliar to consumers without recognizing the vast language gap that has arisen between them. Examples of the many terms which clients have used naively and inappropriately in posing questions to respondents include "blister-pack," "fiber formula," and "tent cards."

Even simple concepts require careful definition to ensure that everyone in the study—respondents who supply the data and analysts who interpret it—are talking about the same things. One of the most common examples is the correct classification of retail outlets, a problem that arises when marketers wish to know where consumers shop. The term "mass merchandiser" or "discount drugstore" may speak volumes to marketers but little to consumers; and anyone who has ever explored the shadowy borders between "speed" and "convenience," or "cream" and "ointment" knows that selecting simple, unambiguous terms can stump even the best questionnnaire draftsmen.

It is wrong to suppose that such problems are a result of consumer ignorance or unsophistication, and that sophisticated respondents can be expected to have less difficulty with terminology. Rather, these ambiguities reflect the remarkable flexibility of common usage and the variety of experiences or perspectives that can distance even sophisticated product users from the marketers who serve them.

For example, it is usually prudent to define drug classes, even for physicians, because without explicit agreement on key terms, survey research can lay little claim to statistical reliability or validity.

Experience suggests that not all physicians will agree on the antihypertensive drugs that fall under the heading, "centrally acting," so a researcher who wishes to learn the image of that drug class should be aware that not all respondents are actually evaluating the same drugs. Group interviews have saved us many times from the consequences of such problems.

Group interviews have also helped us to provide answer categories that reflect real world perceptions and behavior in a way we might otherwise have overlooked. In one study that attempted to determine the incidence of toxicities associated with a particular cardiovascular drug, our first impulse was to ask physicians for numbers of patients believed to be at each (toxic) blood level. We discovered in preliminary groups, however, that physicians may pay far less attention to blood levels than to clinical symptoms and treatment requirements, for example, the need for hospitalization or the need for a pacemaker if the patient becomes extremely toxic. Therefore, the questionnaire was designed around physicians' responses to patient symptoms rather than blood chemistry levels, and as a result, our measurements were significantly more meaningful.

Qualitative research also helps us to develop meaningful response categories for questions that might otherwise be left open ended, and this is a service to both client and researcher. Granted, clients may specifically request some open-ended survey questions (for example, "what problems do you anticipate in using this product?" or "why do you prefer this product over any other?") and indeed, there are times when open-ended questions are preferable because answer categories may cue people to respond in ways they otherwise might not.

However, the enthusiasm which many clients have for open-ended survey questions is often misplaced. It has been our experience that when qualitative research has been used to help generate reasonably comprehensive response categories, an "other, specify" option seldom elicits information not already captured in one or more of the closed answers. Moreover, even highly skilled survey interviewers are likely to obtain shallow or ambiguous responses to open-ended questions and at considerable coding effort and expense. In our view, clients are better served when qualitative analysis is used to design a document as tightly structured as possible, leaving each research methodology to do what it does best.

As important as its role in the framing of questions is the contribution that qualitative research makes in identifying product motivations, purchase inducements barriers and other decision-making factors which must ultimately be reflected in survey questions and answer categories. For example, a common component of many surveys is what is sometimes referred to as "problem detection."[1] Marketers who wish to address unmet needs may attempt to identify them buy asking product users to rate both the frequency and importance of various product deficits. For example, owners of vinyl flooring might tell us that tearing occurs infrequently but is viewed as calamitous, while loss of luster is a problem with almost all floors but is only moderately disturbing. Without preliminary qualitative research, it is hard to imagine generating a comprehensive list of such problems.

Similarly, for the many studies which require us to assess the image of competing products or brands, we must select rating dimensions which play an important role in consumer evaluations. It is rare that we embark on research without some basis for developing such lists, but qualitative research can and generally does sensitize us to aspects we might not otherwise have included.

One particularly important way in which qualitative research contributes to surveys is by helping researchers to generate a battery of descriptive statements that becomes the basis for segmentation analysis. The input for the segmentation is ratings signifying level of agreement or disagreement with a series of opinions or belief statements.

It has been our experience that segmentation analysis is most useful when it reflects an orientation toward particular markets and products rather than general personality traits or worldview ("psychographics"). Consequently, if we are engaged in a segmentation study of the greeting card market, we draft a battery of statements which attempt to capture the psychological needs, attitudes and barriers associated with greeting card exchange. Similarly, if we are segmenting the market for hair care products, we generate a series of statements appropriate to that product category. Needless to say, the clarity and validity of any segmentation analysis depends, above all, on the battery of items used to develop it. Only if the statements are comprehensive, sensitive and unambiguous can the segmentation itself be conceptually sound and productive. Thus, the researcher who devises a custom battery for virtually every segmentation project un-

---

[1]Initially developed by Batten, Barton, Durstine & Osborn, Inc.

dertaken depends heavily on qualitative research to become familiar with the range of sentiments and needs expressed by consumers.

Postsurvey Analysis

Another legitimate use of qualitative research is after, rather than before, a survey is conducted. Qualitative analyses can occasionally help to explain surprising or unexpected outcomes or can provide further elaboration on reactions to a new product idea.

Qualitative research is seldom used this way in practice, probably because many surveys are preceded by exploratory depth interviews as a result of which there are many fewer surprises than there might otherwise be. When product concepts are embraced or rejected, researchers can generally recognize and comprehend the reasons.

In addition, we suspect that there is some intuitive resistance among researchers to ending a survey on a qualitative note. Surveys are typically viewed as definitive and conclusive while qualitative research is thought to be provisional, requiring a head count or a tie breaker to give it ultimate legitimacy. Having already conducted a survey, researchers instinctively look upon depth interviews as a step backward rather than a step forward—a violation of the natural order of things in market research.

Our earlier comments about the relative contributions of each methodology should be taken to imply that we emphatically reject that viewpoint. Qualitative research provides one kind of learning, quantitative research another, and we do not see either one as the inevitable arbiter or final step in the research process. While we believe it is usually prudent to begin research with groups because their speed, flexibility, and economy can save more costly errors, we do not hesitate to recommend a qualitative "postscript" when we believe it would be productive.

INDEPENDENT QUALITATIVE RESEARCH

It is customary in the marketing research industry to preface each qualitative report with a caveat which cautions that the analysis to follow is provisional, subject to further validation by quantitative techniques. Clients are reminded that the method is designed to explain how people feel and how they perceive things, rather than to tally how many of them express any particular point of view.

Despite that caution, not all qualitative studies are necessarily followed by a survey. Many are intended to serve as a basis for marketing decisions rather than simply methodological ones. It is legitimate and, indeed, often desirable to use qualitative research in this manner, providing the limitations are understood and the results are prudently applied. Here are some key examples:

General Education

It is periodically useful for marketing managers to "return to the well" for firsthand exposure to the people who buy their products. Even with a wealth of syndicated purchase data on hand, marketers can easily become estranged from the audience they serve and may incorrectly assume that their own priorities are shared by people who buy and use their products. An example of that parochialism is the marketing manager who believes consumers will surely know cosmetic products are alcohol free simply because alcohol is not printed on the label; or the radio program director who assumes that all editorials are closely and consciously evaluated by listeners when large segments of the audience claim not to care about them. Again, periodic excursions into the market—and particularly, the opportunity to hear consumers speak firsthand—can revitalize and authenticate a client's perceptions of the marketplace more effectively than large numbers or projectable statistics.

Idea Generation

One of the most common ways of using independent qualitative studies is to help generate lists of problems, unmet needs, or ideas for new products which may be turned over to marketing managers or R&D personnel for further consideration. It is generally inappropriate or premature to quantify such data because the raw ideas generated in these sessions are underdeveloped and require further screening and refinement.

The principal shortcomings of idea-generating sessions is their often limited payoff. It is a truism of marketing research that consumers or end users are generally uncreative in directing us toward new products. In some cases, they may even be insensitive to their own problems, having accommodated themselves for so long to something unsatisfactory. In general, however, this type of qualitative research can be grist for the mill and may be utilized without fear that the raw material is statistically unsupported.

Concept Development and Screening

One of the most widely used applications of qualitative research is to help clients and their agencies set directions for creative development by testing and refining trial concepts in group settings. Whether the trial concepts represent new product ideas, alternative product positionings or rough ad executions, they do not necessarily warrant a survey since they are not finished products or end points but steps along the way.

In a similar vein, it is often useful to submit several alternative concepts to respondents as a basis for deciding how much of a company's resources should be allocated to further development or what sort of priority an idea should receive. In a case such as this, it is important to develop a set of criteria for making decisions which observe the limits of qualitative analysis.

By way of example, a company may decide that if a particular product idea is to be successful, it must be viewed by end users as universally standard equipment rather than a specialty item for a narrow market segment. Or the company may conclude that to justify further development, a product must be able to expect heavy or routine use within its target segment. Qualitative research can help clients make those decisions by offering them a laboratory view of the way some users react to the concepts before substantial investments are made. Heavy resistance in, perhaps, four groups does not necessarily predict similar attitudes throughout the broader population, but objections which surface in depth interviews can alert us to potentially serious product deficiencies and encourage some interim reevaluation before additional dollars are spent in marketing research or R&D.

The next example illustrates how discoveries made in group interviews may lead to a reconsideration of product design or positioning. A new product concept designed to relieve gastrointestinal illness was presented to primary care physicians for preliminary evaluation. What distinguished this product from others was the fact that the dosage prescribed was dependent on the precise site in the gastrointestinal tract that was causing distress. General practitioners rejected the new product because it violated the way in which they diagnosed and treated stomach irritation. It was discovered that they rarely conduct tests to determine the site of the discomfort because currently available drugs effectively treat both sites with the same dosage regimen. The client promptly recognized the marketing handicap of a site-dependent dosage schedule and returned the product to the laboratory for futher development. A survey was not necessary or appropriate at that stage.

Similarly, it may be enough to know that some consumers find an ad concept or a product description confusing if what we are seeking is broad comprehension. The actual numbers in such cases may be irrelevant. It is the mere existence of an issue or a problem, and not its prevalence, that concerns us.

Tests of Clarity or Comprehension

One of the most effective applications of qualitative research, and one for which there is no entirely satisfactory substitute, is its use in determining the comprehensibility of consumer-oriented (or professionally-targeted) written materials. We have had occasion to conduct numerous studies in which respondents were asked to preview contract language, brochures, and even book manuscripts prior to publication, and those studies have alerted us to instances in which the materials were ambiguous, obscure, threatening, poorly organized or overstated. While we can conceive of using surveys to test for general comprehension, surveys do not provide sufficient information to pinpoint problem areas and guide editorial improvement.

One of the more intriguing variations on basic applications is mock trials in which litigants present and defend their case before jurors and hire a moderator to help them learn how the arguments were interpreted, received and evaluated. These are being used with increasing frequency to help attorneys develop more coherent presentations, edit or forego evidentary materials that bore or confuse jurors, and manage their own presentation to gain sympathy rather than provoke antagonism.

Opinion Leader Panels

An interesting and rewarding use of qualitative research, especially group interviews, is to assemble leading influentials in a field and present a set of topics for guided discussion. The procedures usually differ slightly from those followed in conventional group interviews. For example, the discussion may last a full day, and it may be held in a resort to encourage leading authorities from all over the country (or the world) to attend. Newer teleconferencing facilities make it possible to obtain some of the benefits of group interaction among authoritative participants unable to meet in the same city. The sponsor's identity is frequently known to participants.

The goals of such a study may or may not include explicit marketing or promotional objectives. The client may simply wish to know how influentials feel about key issues in their field and what future trends are foreseen in order to develop general guidelines for strategic planning. Alternatively, transcripts of the discussion may be made available to others in the field (for example, published in a medical journal) as a promotional gesture.

Opinion leader panels are one application of the group interview which cannot be duplicated using any other methodology. In fact, issues like sampling reliability or projectability are generally moot in such instances because participants represent a relatively small and select group of influentials and may themselves constitute a census of the population we aim to interview.

IMPROPER USES OF QUALITATIVE RESEARCH

Having spent a good deal of time enumerating the legitimate uses of qualitative research, we owe a few words on how groups ought not to be used. It has already been emphasized that qualitative research, for all its virtues and flexibility, is not a sound basis for statistical projection and should not be used to forecast product trial, market share, penetration or other hard measures of market acceptance. In general, we find that most users of qualitative research understand and respect that limitation.

More recently, however, we have observed another serious misuse and abuse of qualitative research, one that is more ethical and practical than statistical in nature. We are referring to the increasing use of so-called "peer influence" or "sales groups" in which respondents, typically professionals and especially people deemed influential in their local community or institution, are invited to group interviews for the express purpose of selling them a product rather than merely learning of their reactions to it. We emphatically reject this concept.

It need hardly be said that invitations extended under false pretenses under "cover" of research objectives violate generally held ethics of the research community. Sales efforts should always be made explicit because respondents who willingly or enthusiastically attend group interviews might not choose to participate in sessions motivated by sales objectives. We find that group participants are generally motivated not only by the promise of a financial incentive but also by their genuine interest in conversing with other colleagues and offering their personal views to manufacturers and marketers. For some, the premium we offer is less compensation or reward than permission; it allows people, especially busy professionals, to do something they enjoy without feeling abused or undervalued.

Some have argued that a peer influence group is legitimate so long as the agenda is made explicit in advance, and we cannot refute the ethics of that premise. We do, however, question its long-term practical implications for the marketing research community as a whole. When moderators and research organizations lend their auspices, their facilities, and their time to selling efforts, there is some risk that their image of dispassion and professional integrity may ultimately be eroded. A physician who has been present at a sales group may always suspect the loyalties or goals of the moderator or sponsoring research firm. Even if disclaimers to the contrary are made in subsequent group sessions, neutrality is a mantle not easily discarded and reassumed. Moreover, growing research expenditures mean that increasing demands are being made on the time and good will of respondent populations, including both consumers and professional groups. Given those demands, cynicism and mistrust are attitudes the marketing research community can ill afford to cultivate.

We have a slightly different set of reservations about the use of group interview videotapes as a source of promotional "clips." Although no ethical issues are raised if respondents are duly informed, the explicit prospect that excerpts may be used to promote a product is liable to diminish the candor of the discussion, either by discouraging criticism or by encouraging more fulsome praise. In general, a study which sets out to serve both masters—data-gathering and promotion—serves neither one very well. Thus, clients who are serious about either objective would probably do well to address them separately.

Design
of Group Interview
Studies

Chapter 4

It is widely assumed that group interview studies are less expensive than surveys. For that reason, they are not necessarily designed with the same care as surveys, on the belief that the risks and penalties of error are substantially smaller.

While the cost per study of group interview projects is often less than surveys, the cost per respondent (ranging from $300 to $500) is actually far higher. With that view in mind, it is perhaps wise to review many of the research orthodoxies that guide group configuration and encourage a more careful and deliberate approach to the design process.

The first section of this chapter, Configuring Groups, considers who should be interviewed, how many groups and moderators are optimal, how groups should be structured, and in how many locations they should be conducted. The second section, Respondent Preparation, discusses what kinds of preparation should be required of respondents prior to the group's information.

CONFIGURING GROUPS

In qualitative research, just as in other types of studies, ambitious research goals often defer to budget limitations. In fact, many qualitative study

designs reflect research needs and cost considerations in nearly equal measure, and that is probably as it should be. Researchers often view group
interviews as a less expensive alternative to surveys. While that may be a
misconception, group interview studies can often withstand compromises
better than most surveys because they do not bear the burden of statistical
reliability.

Cost constraints are not all bad, since they impose a discipline on the
design process. Tight budgets force clients to conceptualize their needs
carefully and to prioritize, sometimes even abandon, peripheral goals. Indeed, it might be argued that one regrettable luxury of generous budgets is
undisciplined thinking.

An obvious point that bears repetition is the importance of carefully
reviewing study objectives with the client at the outset. In some instances,
subtle but significant issues may be obscured by rather global generalities in
the client's research agenda. An individual with the aim of learning how to
build a radio audience may be concerned principally about competitive
stations within the same format or may want to understand how listeners
can be attracted from other formats, even from other media. A client who
wants to learn more about the prospects for a new medical instrument may,
on close consideration, be concerned about acceptance by physicians, medical distributors, patients, or some combination of all those groups. Questions like those have implications for respondent selection, so it is essential
that the researcher explore carefully with clients at the outset what they
wish to learn about which segments of the market.

Equally important in designing a study is the need to explore with the
client what information is already available and what questions remain
unanswered. Clients sometimes claim to know a great deal about their
market but on close insepction, the researchers may discover that the information is outdated, unreliable or based more on hunch and prejudice than
reality.

For example, clients may rely for information on the company sales
representatives, who bring a useful but not entirely disinterested perspective to marketing issues. Conversely, clients sometimes conclude that they
need "new" data bacause previous studies have been unable to help them
solve intractible marketing problems. A revisit is often appropriate although unnecessary replications can be disappointing to all concerned.

Therefore, it is the job of the researcher to review carefully with the
client what has already been discovered through prior research, which
elements of that data base require updating or expansion, and which questions are as yet unanswered. (What to do when those questions exceed the
available time and budget is addressed in a later chapter.) Assuming, however, that there is agreement on the study agenda and the resources available to cover it, the first and most important design question is who to
interview.

WHO SHOULD BE INTERVIEWED?

The number of group sessions conducted, the types of respondents interviewed, and the actual composition of each group are all interdependent
design elements, and no one decision can be made without reference to
another. Nevertheless, the first step in developing a research design (once
key research issues have been identified) is to enumerate all of the respondent categories one wishes to represent in the study and particularly those
for whom quotas are to be specified.

Age, sex, income and purchase behavior are among the most common building blocks of any sampling plan, but practical limitations (that is,
the relatively small number of respondents in a qualitative study) often
dictate that some be assigned more or less importance than others or occasionally be disregarded entirely.

To illustrate the point, consider a floor covering manufacturer who
wishes to understand the factors that shape flooring purchase. As researchers, we might opt to interview any one of the following: (1) women
who have owned or lived with particular types of flooring, (2) women who
intend to purchase new flooring in the near future, (3) women who have
already begun shopping for new flooring, or (4) women who have already
purchased new floors. The manufacturer might also consider enlisting
some men in his sample in acknowledgement that men are often individual
homeowners or may share home decorating responsibilities with their
partners.

From among all these groups, it is imperative that we select respondents whose comments will be most relevant and most informative. The
group process is, after all, not a ballot by which to survey the entire marketplace but rather a prism through which we focus our attention and gather
rich and detailed information from a relatively limited number of relevant
individuals.

The basic rule of thumb in selecting respondents is to determine the
types of individuals who are most representative of the target market. In
the flooring illustration, it might be argued that while every head of household is a potential customer at some point in the future, individuals who
have already made a commitment to purchase new floors, and particularly
those who have already visited a store or made a purchase, will be more
attuned to the needs and motivations driving their behavior and better able
to articulate the dynamics of the purchasing process. On those grounds, we
might decide to exclude women who are not yet ready to purchase new
flooring and for whom the entire subject is probably not very salient. In
other words, respondents with recent, relevant experience even if they are
technically no longer "in" the market, are often the most informative.

Using the same line of reasoning, we might argue that however much
men and women may be sharing or exchanging traditional roles in our

society, this particular product category still falls squarely under the jursidiction of women in most households, with men tending to ratify, rather than govern, purchase decisions.

In excluding certain respondent categories from our qualitative research, we are not arguing that they are entirely irrelevant or that we could never expect to learn anything productive by speaking with them. Indeed, we might very well choose to include them in a follow-up survey sample where large numbers give greater sampling latitude. Since, however, qualitative research should be designed to focus attention on the most relevant issues and the most promising markets, it is advisable to define the universe carefully, even narrowly, in order to maximize the yield of information.

Having decided that the relevant universe is represented by women who are either about to purchase flooring or have recently done so, and having determined how we wish to operationalize those criteria, our next responsibility is to decide in what proportions to recruit these women and what other subgroups, if any, should be quota sampled. For this purpose, we apply the second rule of thumb: Which types of respondents do we intend to single out for separate analysis?

In this case, we may wish to set quotas on equal numbers of recent and intended purchasers, since women who have already purchased new flooring may have tempered their expectations and even their preferences after the fact. If we expect that recent and intended purchasers are different in some ways and that those differences are potentially informative, we will want to retain the flexibility of analyzing them separately.

Of course, in some studies, it is important to represent attitudinal segments rather than merely behavioral groups. In a study of low-fat dairy products, we recruited several groups of respondents who considered themselves to be conscious of health or nutrition and operationalized that definition with attitude and behavior questions in the screener.

In most studies, we are likely to consider the relevance of demographic characteristics such as age and income, as well as behavior or attitudes. While age is often a relevant marketing parameter, we might decide here that income is more germane, since it directs women toward particular types and grades of flooring on the basis of higher or lower price points. Thus, we might choose to represent women from two or three income categories and permit age to distribute itself naturally within some upper and lower bounds.

If this were a typical study, we would by now have also given thought to regional stratification and probably opted to schedule groups in at least two different parts of the country. We would like, however, to reserve discussion of region for a later section, since it usually has greater cost implications than any other variable although its methodological importance in qualitative research is sometimes overstated.

HOW MANY GROUPS TO CONDUCT?

Although we have already identified several variables of interest in our hypothetical flooring project (purchase behavior, income and region), we have not yet made a decision on the number of groups to include or the way to structure them. If one analogizes the design process to computing a set of equations with three unknowns—the type of respondents, the number of groups and the composition of those groups—it becomes apparent that once any two of these issues have been resolved, there is little uncertainty remaining about the third.

As we noted earlier, a realistic researcher takes some account of budget when he specifies the number of groups to be conducted. However, there are few, if any, universal precepts to guide the design process because there are no objective or statistical standards by which to measure the adequacy of a qualitative study. Researchers seeking quantifiable data recognize that surveys of fewer than 100 respondents tend to be cost-inefficient, and that subgroups of less than 35 are statistically unstable. The qualitative researcher, however, is thrust back upon experience, judgment and intuition when making decisions on the number of groups because statistical significance and sample size are irrelevant.

At best, there is, or probably should be, general agreement that it is unwise to conduct only a single group, unless that group is thought to be uniquely respresentative of the relevant universe and cannot be duplicated (for example, a set of leading medical authorities or a company's regional sales force). The rationale is practical rather than theoretical: For a relatively small incremental cost, we obtain the benefit of some added diversity and a steep moderator learning curve. Admittedly, however, this same argument could be made on behalf of three groups or even more, and indeed, we would have to acknowledge that four groups are generally better or safer than two. Where, then, should the line be drawn and how is the decision made?

The number of groups conducted should bear a rough relationship to the number of respondent variables we wish to investigate. If we plan to compare the roles of age, sex, and income, we will need a larger number of groups to accommodate our analysis. At some point, however, diminishing returns begin to set in, and it is the responsibility of the researchers to anticipate that point in each study they design.

Our experience suggests that most research issues can be addressed satisfactorily with no more than six or eight groups and that four are often entirely adequate. We discourage any more than ten in a single wave because the additional groups seldom contribute new insights. In addition, the cost and time required for such protracted studies tend to offset some of the advantages of qualitative research without making the findings any more statistically projectable.

Clients new to qualitative research or inherently mistrustful of the methodology sometimes ask, "How can you presume to tell me about my market on the basis of only 36 people (that is, four groups)?" As we have already noted, the answer depends on what they wish to learn. In qualitative research, each respondent serves as a window on many points of view—those he or she personally takes ownership of and those that have been rejected. Surveys tend to streamline ideas so that they can be counted. Qualitative studies look for the broader ideological motivational complexities that elude other methods. In that sense, each group respondent is, as one of our colleagues has aptly put it, a microcosm of his or her universe, and it may not matter whether we explore 36 or 45 of those microcosms.

HOW SHOULD GROUPS BE STRUCTURED AND WHAT TYPES OF RESPONDENTS SHOULD BE SEGREGATED FROM ONE ANOTHER?

In designating the number of groups and the structure of each, an important decision is whether to segregate key subgroups from one another—for example, users and nonusers—or to combine them in a single session. There is a tendency for many researchers to segregate dissimilar respondents on grounds that (1) it might otherwise be difficult to distinguish them in the analysis, and (2) respondents with different backgrounds or viewpoints may intimidate and restrain one another.

While there is sometimes merit in the first argument, we take issue with the second. In point of fact, it is often useful to invite respondents with differing viewpoints to confront one another because we learn a great deal about the strength of convictions and the magnitude of attitude differences when beliefs are tested in a group setting.

This is not to suggest that certain demographic or behavioral groups cannot, or should not, be segregated in group interviews. It is generally wise to at least consider separating respondents whose differences carry strong implications of social, economic, or professional status—differences which might promote an artificial hierarchy that discourages candor or penalizes disagreement.

We might, for example, choose to separate high income respondents from those who are more downscale *if*—and this is an important condition—we expect the product behavior under discussion to reflect income differences in a significant way. For example, we would probably choose to separate lower and upper income respondents in a group discussion on travel packages or jewelry, where income-related price sensitivity is anticipated. Similarly, we almost always segregate general practitioners from medical specialists, or top management representatives from other management strata, because experience suggests that the implied status differences, as well as the very real differences in professional training and job description, usually make separate sessions more productive. One exception to that general principle is in the investigation of how conflicting perceptions and values tend to be accommodated or resolved when different professional groups interact with one another.

By contrast, we would probably not segregate respondents on the basis of income in a study of deodorant or soft drinks. In less costly, more pedestrian product categories, the relationship between income and price sensitivity is often obscured by other overriding habits and product preferences.

In sum, the study objectives and the product category generally ought to determine how groups are configurated and which sets of respondents should be shielded from whom. However, several demographic variables, namely sex and race, deserve special mention in this regard.

Sex

Traditionally men and women have been segregated in group interviews on the assumptions that (1) men and women are often fundamentally different in their motivations and perceptions, (2) sexual embarrassment or vanity might dampen conversation, or certainly inhibit candor, and (3) traditional sex roles would elevate men to positions of dominance in the groups and discourage women from contributing equally, or would produce some unwanted courtship behavior that might subvert the research goals.

All of these concerns may have once been valid but social observation and actual research experience indicate that these issues are far less relevant now than they were 20 years ago. Today, it is largely inertia and research ritual which perpetuate an automatic segregation of the sexes in almost all group interview projects.

Actually, we see little compelling reason to abandon this general strategy since it is seldom harmful. Indeed, some product categories continue to require it. One would not, for example, choose to include both men and women in a group interview on beer because beer is a traditional symbol of fellowship and masculinity, and even women tend to grant men a proprietary role in this product category.

For similar reasons, it is probably desirable to segregate men and women in discussions of toiletry products, even items like soap or toothpaste, on the assumption that sexual equality has done nothing to erase sexual embarrassment or vanity. Sensitive issues like breath and body odor or bathing and grooming are probably best discussed in the relative privacy and security of single sex groups.

On the other hand, while qualitative researchers sometimes worry that women may be dominated or outranked by male colleagues in professional group sessions, we find this concern to be unfounded. Female professionals at all levels and in every field from medicine to retail sales are speaking out in group sessions without apparent fear of male rejection or disapproval.

Even in consumer categories, it may be entirely appropriate to mix men and women as long as both sexes are actually involved in the shopping process. One important factor which will continue to discourge the inclusion of both men and women in the same group interview is their tradtionally different roles in the selection and purchase of many product categories. While household roles are generally far more flexible and less traditional than in the past, many families still assign positions of implied shopping dominance to one or the other member, and these often reflect vestigial sex roles. Thus, we find that women tend to be primary food decision makers more often than men (even in households where men may be dispatched to do the actual purchasing), and men still remain key customers for hardware and household tools.

Even men who assume a dominant role in food shopping or cooking may tend, on historic grounds, to defer to women in mixed sessions, and for that reason, segregation may still be prudent. It is often entirely appropriate, however, to mix single (solo dwelling) men and women, since all are presumably responsible for everyday activity of their own households. We have found these combinations to interact very well in topics dealing with everything from investment and banking to snack foods.

Over the years, we have also had occasion to invite the participation of husband and wife pairs in joint sessions in order to explore the decision-making process surrounding purchases in which both spouses are actively involved. Examples include major investment purchases like homes and cars. Our judgment is that these sessions are generally limited in their value. The deficit in such groups is that we actually halve the number of independent observations while not necessarily obtaining additional insight on how intramural differences or competing priorities are actually resolved at the time of purchase. It is a technique to be used sparingly and with conservative expectations.

Race and Ethnicity

It is our general policy to invite group diversity by mixing blacks and whites in the same sessions unless a study specifically focuses on black consumers or they constitute so important and specialized a segment of the product category that their views and experiences warrant separate analysis. Examples of the former include studies designed to explore the impact of black participation in product advertising; examples of the latter would include studies of malt liquor, a product category in which blacks have traditionally accounted for a disproportionate share of volume.

Most clients have become increasingly sensitive to the importance of Hispanic marketing programs and in these studies, language considerations may argue for segregating Spanish-speaking respondents. Under ordinary circumstances, however, English-speaking Hispanics may be included in consumer groups on a more random basis (like Italians or Irish) with no hope or expectation of singling them out for separate analysis. It goes almost without saying that ethnic and income variables are often confounded, but in our experience, most studies either stratify groups by income or set a minimum eligibility level so that impoverished respondents are not represented. (The appropriateness of that restriction can certainly be argued in many product categories but it is not entirely without justification. People *may* be more realistic and articulate in their product assessments if they are better able to afford them.)

We have found, however, that when we want to reflect class in group recruiting (for example "Yuppies"), it is generally wise to take education as well as income into account since class is a multidimensional stratification system, and blue-collar workers often earn higher incomes than college graduates.

HOW MANY LOCATIONS?

One of the key issues to address in designing a qualitative study is where to conduct the groups, a design factor with significant implications for both the number of groups and the cost of the project. Because there is usually some temptation to replicate groups across several regions, the number of sites selected is often the multiplier which actually determines the ultimate size of the study.

It seems to us that the role and importance of region is widely misunderstood and therefore overstated in some studies. With that in mind, we propose to review the value and the limitations of regional stratification.

Above all, the purpose of conducting qualitative research in more than one location is to ensure that the data we have collected are not idiosyncratic to a particular community. Like the broad socioeconomic mix we aim for in most group sessions, regional dispersion is a safety check that contributes to group diversity *without necessarily affording us an opportunity for systematic regional comparison.* This last disclaimer is important because no qualitative design, even one reflecting four or five different regions, can be said to represent America. If vivid cross-regional contrasts do present themselves, they should still be viewed cautiously as the possible product of chance rather than region per se. This same caveat applies to any variable we study in a qualitative analysis, including sex and income.

Moreover, in a population as geographically mobile as ours, the relationship between location and region is frequently diluted. We often find, for example, that a group of so-called Southerners in Atlanta or Dallas includes at least three or four recent emigres from the North who have not yet been assimilated into their new regional culture.

Where hunch or avilable market data suggest that region may have strong implications for the research findings, some cautious comparisons can legitimately be attempted. By way of example, if a particular brand or product category is known to perform well in some communities and poorly in others (the use of microwaves, for example, has grown more rapidly in the West than elsewhere), one goal of the research may be to shed light on those regional differences by selecting sites accordingly. In general, however, it is wise to look upon geographic representation in groups as an additional instrument for achieving diversity rather than a tool for systematically analyzing it.

A typical study may require groups in no more than two or three locations and certainly no more than four. Convenience (namely, the availability of facilities and airline flights) often directs qualitative researchers toward major metropolitan areas. A good case can be made for occasionally straying from large cities to achieve greater diversity, but if a community is truly off the beaten track, moderator and observers will have to forego the creature comforts of group rooms, one-way mirrors and first-rate audio equipment.

Are there circumstances in which it is legitimate to conduct groups in only one location? The answer is yes, principally in situations like these:

1. The groups are meant to provide preliminary guidance to creative team members in generating material for later testing.

2. The groups are designed as a check on action taken as a result of more extensive prior research, for example, the revision of concept boards or a change in labeling.

3. The study is intended to support questionnaire development so that quantitative analyses by region will be possible later.

4. Sales data suggest that regional variations in behavior tend to be trivial.

HOW MANY RESPONDENTS IN A GROUP?

There is widespread agreement that the optimal number of respondents per group is between eight and ten. As a result, the issue is seldom explicitly raised in designing qualitative studies. The question is more likely to arise when the designated quota of respondents was not achieved and as a result, those who commissioned or conducted the groups have reason to question whether a group interview, in the true sense of the term, actually took place.

The rationale for enlisting eight to ten respondents is fundamentally a practical one. Experience suggests that this number provides a diversity of views and the benefits of interaction without seriously curtailing the participation of any of the members. Occasionally, zealous recruiting or accident results in a full house (11 or 12 participants), and while it is certainly possible to conduct a group with that many people, the moderator should not attempt to solicit participation from all. In two brief hours, respondents cannot learn to interact with an unlimited number of new acquaintances; neither can the moderator give all of them the attention they require. Beyond a certain number of participants, less is definitely more.

Extra respondents who have taken the trouble to come may actually be irritated or disappointed to be given their premiums and sent home, but it is also unfair to accommodate the overflow if it means that participants will be pressed uncomfortably together for a two-hour period. The moderator must exercise judgment as the situation requires.

An embarrassment of riches may be unwelcome in group recruiting, but what of the more disconcerting problem: a group with too few respondents? It is possible to conduct a productive group with as few as five, since that number is adequate to provide some breadth of opinion and spur general interaction. Indeed, if five respondents ever seem uncomfortable in a group interview room, it is often because of the moderator has communicated to them some anxiety or disappointment that more are not present. When fewer than five respondents participate, we collect what information we can but generally resign ourselves to conducting a make-up group.

There are, however, circumstances under which a mini-group is actually desirable, for example, if there is only a small number of eligible respondents in the community and it is desirable to bring them together for the sake of interaction, or if the agenda is limited and there seems little reason to enlist a full complement of participants. In those cases, we may actively recruit only five on the assumption that benefits of the group process can be obtained at lower cost and/or greater efficiency than with a series of individual interviews. We do take issue with the use of dyadic interviews, the simultanaeous interviewing of a pair of respondents, because in our view, this arrangement does not offer the benefits of *either* group *or* individual interviews and brings no unique advantages of its own.

HOW MANY MODERATORS?

One issue that frequently arises in planning a group study is the appropriateness of dividing the groups between two or more moderators. Scheduling conflicts sometimes raise this issue for consideration and we believe that the number of moderators who are invited to participate in the study should, quite simply, relate to the number of groups actually conducted.

When a study involves four or six groups, it is usually desirable to have only one moderator conduct them all unless the second moderator is present for the first set and can advance on the learning curve along with the first moderator. The initial group in any study is something of a dry run in which the moderator learns how the conversation tends to be sequenced, what issues surface spontaneously and which ones need careful probing, which techniques work best at eliciting subtle insights and how the session should be paced. Subsequent groups are generally more productive because the moderator knows better what to expect and, having interacted with client observers, is better able to direct succeeding groups in a way that addresses the client's requirements.

When, however, there are eight or more groups, a strong argument can be made for purposely dividing the work between two moderators. Beyond six groups, the learning curve not only levels off, it may actually dip as repetition and fatigue desensitize even a conscientious moderator.

Another benefit of dividing the work between two moderators is the prospect of gaining different professional perspectives on the same research effort. The interaction between two (or more) moderators may greatly enrich the insights that emerge from a method that is so dependent on moderator experience and creative interpretation. For that reason, two individuals may occasionally co-moderate a group session, although the success of that procedure generally requires that, like trapeze artists, the moderators know each other well enough to maintain necessary balance.

WHO SHOULD BE EXCLUDED FROM GROUPS?

It is customary to exclude certain types of respondents whose involvement in the category or whose prior participation in qualitative research may somehow diminish or distort their contributions. These restrictions can be reconsidered and either modified or abandoned if unusual circumstances (for example, a dearth of eligible respondents) argue for greater latitude in recruiting. The following sections offer suggested guidelines.

Repeat Participants

Researchers do what they can to minimize gratuitous differences between respondents and the universe they purport to represent. Frequent participation is one basis for doing so. Therefore, it is common to require that respondents accepted for a group must not have participated in a prior session during the past six to twelve months. This stipulation is designed to screen out "professional respondents," those individuals who, for love or money, may attend groups as often as several times per month.

There are many sensible reasons for excluding professional respondents. First, there is concern that such individuals are different from others who do not make a habit of group participation. Actually, we suspect that those differences have few implications for their consumer behavior as long as the respondents do not dissemble or misrepresent themselves. Unfortunately, an individual who seeks out opportunities for group participation, whether motivated by money or sheer diversion (and we have seen both operating) may be sorely tempted to lie about his or her behavior in order to qualify for admission. Screening forms are designed to minimize that risk but it would be unrealistic to assume that screening forms are always administered in precisely the way we wish them to be or that dedicated repeaters will candidly admit to previous participation when questioned. Whatever the controls, some repeat participants probably do find their way into many groups, and while their presence is undesirable, we suspect that they do relatively little damage. However, every reasonable effort should be made to apply eligibility criteria rigorously and to identify failures in the screening process.

Another concern is that repeat respondents may, by virtue of frequent exposure, become familiar with group moderating techniques and attempt to manipulate them or anticipate what they believe are desired responses. Pseudosophistication of this sort is unwelcome because it generally precludes candor. Even fresh respondents may attempt this sort of second-guessing or subversion, but there may be greater risk that the professional respondent will attempt to exercise "professional" skills in a disruptive or ingenuous way. There is also greater risk that repeat participants will mistake their proper role and attempt to serve as marketing experts or consultants. This behavior, though meant to be helpful, is generally unwelcome.

Occasionally, it may actually be desirable to have seasoned, repeat participants if what we want is a panel of unusually creative or articulate individuals. Under those circumstances, however, we are fully cognizant that the respondents have been chosen for their exceptional qualitites, not necessarily for their representativeness and we must draw conclusions with that caveat in mind.

People Connected with Marketing Research or Advertising

It is also customary to eliminate repondents from groups or surveys if they or members of their immediate families are employed in marketing research or advertising. The assumption here is that individuals with some link to those fields may be biased by their proximity to marketing or, on rare occasions, may violate the security of a study by revealing test concepts to competitors.

The true value of this screen may be limited, but since it serves to exlude relatively few individuals, this custom can safely be followed except in cases where extremely low incidence argues against almost any sample restrictions.

People Employed in the Industry Being Studied

It goes almost without saying that people employed in the industry under study, or their close relatives, should be excluded from group interviews. Their special circumstances make them unrepresentative of ordinary consumers and, again, may result in a security violation. Their attitudes are often biased by firsthand knowledge of the industry and their purchase behavior may be atypical because of special discounts or information not widely available.

In setting recruiting specifications, the researcher must decide how narrowly or broadly to draw the boundaries of exclusion. For example, when recruiting respondents for groups on carbonated soft drinks, it is common to exclude not only employees and relatives of manufacturers, bottlers, and distributors, but also people with a link to the wholesale or retail grocery business. It might be argued that individuals who work in the grocery business have access to information or to discounts which make their views and experiences atypical. These decisions must always be made on a case-by-case basis, but given the relatively small number of respondents in qualitative studies, the wise course is usually the conservative one: When in doubt, leave them out.

People Already Well Acquainted with One Another or with the Moderator

Researchers generally prefer that groups of people already acquainted with one another not be invited to the same session. Objections to the practice of assembling friends in a group session are based on concerns that prior relationships may alter the process by which group cohesion and interaction develop. When people have developed a previous pattern of interacting with one another, there is some likelihood that they will assume those same roles in the group discussion with the accompanying risk that one will speak on behalf of the other or that the two will strive for consensus. We seek to avoid these situations for much the same reason that we do not normally interview members of the same families (unless we wish explicitly to compare their responses), and that is because it is desirable to minimize response interdependence. Ultimately, the very process of interaction in a group session forges roles and relationships which do imply domination/subordination and hierarchy. We usually prefer that these evolve *during* the session.

These arguments make a persuasive case against inviting club chapters or other preexisting social mirocosms (unless there is some explicit desire to interview those particular groups), but it does not necessarily rule out inviting pairs of individuals. Indeed, it is sometimes argued that pairs of friends or acquaintances will feel more socially relaxed in the group setting and more inclined to participate fully. In addition, friends may actually expose one another's deceptions. For example, a beer drinker who claimed to drink only one six-pack per week was challenged by a friend with the reminder that he had consumed more than that the previous weekend.

Most persuasive, however, is the need in some communities to minimize security risks and encourage attendance when group location or timing discourages women from coming unescorted. And of course, we make no attempt to enforce rules about prior acquaintance when inviting groups of professionals such as physicians from the same community, since many or most will already know one another.

One should, however, take special pains to avoid inviting participants who have a prior personal or social relationship with the moderator, since their presence imposes a burden on both parties to camouflage the relationship. It also creates opportunities for conflict or cross-purpose which jeopardize the group as a whole. The controlled self-presentation of the moderator—his or her freedom to direct or stage-manage events during the group—can easily be compromised by an individual who knows the moderator "backstage" and whose presence may consciously or unconsciously distort the moderator's behavior.

There may be circumstances under which it is desirable for market researchers to solicit information from people they know well but those interviews should always be conducted on an individual basis. Whatever biases or distortions are introduced can then be contained and corrected without doing damage to an entire group.

RESPONDENT PREPARATION

For most group studies, it is sufficient to identify respondents who have relevant product needs or experiences and invite them to the group without prior preparation or sensitization. A general description of the topic at the time of invitation is all that is required. In some cases, however, it is impossible to recruit individuals with relevant experience, perhaps because the product is not yet marketed or some very specialized or intensified product exposure is required for meaningful analysis. When that occurs, procedures must be devised to compensate for sampling limitations or to otherwise heighten respondent sensitivity so that the groups are more productive.

Prior Concept Exposure

Because some concepts are so difficult to convey, it is unrealistic to introduce them in a group setting and expect thoughtful and meaningful responses. For example, in one study designed to gauge consumer response to Universal Life Insurance prior to its initial market introduction, the complexity of the concept was such that consumers could not have been expected to grasp it in the space of a group interview. It was necessary to send descriptive materials in advance so that the group session could be devoted to information gathering rather than instruction. Had the major focus of the study been to identify sources of confusion in a salesman's oral presentation, then spontaneous reactions would have been quite relevant. However, because the objective of the study was to assess appeal of the concept in order to permit further product refinement, it was crucial that participants thoroughly understand its provisions.

Similar pregroup exposure is particularly effective in presenting technically demanding new product concepts to professionals. For example, physicians have been sent descriptions of pharmaceutical products with dramatically new modes of action and state-of-the-art diagnostic equipment, and corporate telecommunications managers have been sent new systems concepts.

Topic Sensitization

When the topic under discussion centers around routine habits and activities which normally receive little notice, we may ask respondents in advance of the groups to pay them closer attention. This approach may be particularly useful when we are interested in learning the motivations for mundane or ritualized behavior whose significance and rationale have long been lost. It is also useful, perhaps mandatory, when we wish to develop new product ideas on the basis of current unmet needs.

Familiarity breeds resignation, if not contentment, so that over time, people may become oblivious to daily irritations. Therefore, we often find that without prior sensitization, it is difficult for respondents to recognize and unmet needs. Cases in point are the respondents who describe elaborate procedures for mixing their own new products out of two or three existing ones while claiming to be entirely satisfied with what is already available.

Consumers also tend to assume that many small problems simply cannot be solved (for example, floors will always need waxing and cough syrup will always drip), and may feel it is churlish or unrealistic to complain about them. Presensitization addresses all of these issues: It draws attention to pedestrian, nearly invisible routines; it encourages participants to think about the needs and motivations from which these behaviors once sprang; and it impresses upon them that we are in earnest when we urge them to report on *any* problem, no matter how trivial or irresolvable they believe it to be.

One of the most concrete techniques for presensitizing respondents is to distribute customized diaries one or two weeks prior to the groups and ask them to fill them out as directed. (Additional financial incentives may be required to promote the necessary cooperation.) In one study of snack behavior, which is arguably one of the most routine and habitual activities people engage in, respondents were asked to record every snack consumed over a 48-hour period, as well as the time, location, their mood, and other options considered or food preferred but unavailable. In another project, physicians were requested to make note for one full week of every problem or inconvenience encountered during the course of their daily medical practice. In no case did we wish to tally or necessarily even collect the diaries. The goal was merely to stimulate thought and call attention to behaviors and motivations normally obscured by habit or resignation.

Prior Product Experience

In studies in which the focus of exploration is satisfaction with specific products, either those already on the market or working prototypes of new ones, participants must have direct, personal experience in order to make relevant responses. As noted earlier, if a product is widely marketed and the incidence of use is fairly widespread, recruiting specifications can ensure a group whose experience is relevant to the research issues. However, if the product to be tested is not yet marketed, or market penetration is so limited that users are nearly impossible to recruit, direct experience can be guaranteed by requiring participants to buy the product or by distributing the product for use before the group (home placement).

In a study designed to test reactions to three-dimensional still photography, groups were actually convened twice. In the first session, the concept was discussed and actual prints displayed to evaluate reactions to the concept. Participants were then given cameras and film and instructed how to use them. When the prints were processed and returned, the group was reconvened. In the second group, the focus of discussion shifted to performance of the camera, the total procedure by which film was processed and handled, and participants' satisfaction with the prints. Participants were invited to show their prints to others and discuss whatever difficulties emerged in the course of using the camera. This exercise suggested how the user instructions could be improved, what the most acceptable mail-in and return procedures might be, and what product processing enhancements would promote acceptance. Test product distribution is especially common in studies evaluating new food products, where interest in usage experience, and even in the reactions of family members, often require that participants test the product at home either prior to the discussion or between group sessions.

Concurrent Product Experience

When exposure to a product sample is required for evaluation but the product cannot be dispensed prior to the groups, it is sometimes possible to structure the group session so that product experience is as realistic or naturalistic as possible. For example, in a study focusing on the appeal of videoconferencing, business executives were invited to a site in Chicago while the moderator conducted the group from conferencing facilities in Philadelphia. It is difficult to imagine a more relevant or valid technique for assessing product interest. In another such instance, surgeons evaluating a new wound closure method were asked to use the device to close a dummy patient on an operating table. This allowed participants to experience the product in a situation that mimicked live applications, and it allowed the moderator to direct inquiries toward specific aspects of the product's performance.

In consumer studies, group rooms may be modified so that an entire wall is converted to a facsimile of supermarket shelves, and products are displayed as they would be in a store. Participants are given a sum of money to spend and then led into a discussion of what motivated the choice of some products over others. Once again, in simulations of this kind, we expose the selection process to more direct scrutiny and avoid some of the retrospective distortion that occurs when consumers are asked to explain their behavior after the fact.

Procedures like these are not uncommon, but they are required only when respondents cannot be expected to provide meaningful reactions in the space of two hours without some sensitizing experience. In most cases, unprimed or unprepared respondents arrive with all that is required, an understanding that they will be asked for opinions and a willingness to share them with others.

Group Facilities and Their Procedures

Chapter 5

When a researcher selects a group facility, he or she is entrusting that organization with much of the responsibility for the group's ultimate success. As a result, decisions about which facilities to use and how to oversee their activities can become as important as many of the more rarefied methodological decisions that shape the design of the research. This chapter discusses the role of group facilities and how their features and services affect the outcome of group studies.

THE GROUP INTERVIEWING FACILITY

In the early history of group interviewing, groups were typically conducted in hotel meeting rooms. The few hardy moderators prepared to conduct group interviews in out-of-town facilities embarked for the field with an open reel recorder and its attendant cables, cords, microphones and sundry spare parts. Even large cities could rarely provide rooms with viewing mirrors and recording facilities, and the few market research firms or advertising agencies that had their own facilities seldom made them available for rent to outsiders. Typically, the only viewing rooms that could be rented were located in university psychology departments. Today, there are approximately 700 group facilities in the U.S., including many in small cities across the country. This figure is based on a count of group interviewing rooms reported in the *National Directory of Focus Group Discussion Facilities* (1986).

Most full-service research organizations maintain a group room and recruiting capabilities in their home offices but are obliged to rent facilities when conducting groups in other locations. In addition there are many independent moderators who rely entirely on rented facilities to recruit and host sessions. The growth in the number of these group facilities throughout the country may, in fact, be a proxy for the dramatic increase in the number of groups conducted.

Selection of a group facility should reflect a number of considerations, but above all (1) the caliber, integrity, and reliability of the recruiting, (2) the facility's accessibility (to moderator and respondents), and (3) the creature comforts it can provide. Regrettably, it is often necessary to sacrifice one feature in order to obtain another, and of course, in a "one room" town there is no luxury of choice at all.

Good recruiting—the ability to secure an adequate number of correctly screened and eligible respondents—depends not only on the conscientiousness of those managing the facility but equally on the screening materials and the guidelines set for the facility by those managing the project. Before addressing those issues, we would like to begin by outlining the characteristics of a group facility which contribute directly to the success of the interviews and which deserve consideration by those selecting a facility or establishing one of their own.

Location of the Facility

Perhaps the greatest virtue of a well-designed group facility is that it is easy for the participants to locate. Late arrivals have delayed the start of many a group because of difficulty finding the facility. Group rooms in large downtown office buildings or hotels with multiple elevator banks may be a special problem if there are not prominent and explicit directions to the group interview reception area. Professionals and senior executives are especially likely to be annoyed and arrive in a sour, unreceptive mood after wandering around the building.

Also discouraging to respondents and to road-weary moderators are suburban facilities located away from well-marked roads or within a large shopping complex where street addresses alone may provide no guidance. Here, too, explicit directions reduce the risk of a late or lost participant.

All other things being equal, it is often preferable to hold evening consumer groups, particularly groups of women, in suburban facilities since many women are reluctant to venture into downtown areas in the evening and may require additional incentives to pay for parking and/or a longer trip from outlying areas. Of course, other considerations may argue for a downtown facility (such as the size of viewing facilities or the caliber of recruiting). However if a downtown facility is selected, it is wise to pursue the organization's track record before entrusting it with evening groups of women.

Layout

The interviewing environment While the physical environment in which the group is conducted generally contributes little to the ultimate usefulness of the data, a poorly structured or managed facility can become intrusive enough to distract the moderator, participants, or observers, and it can directly undermine the success of the groups.

To illustrate the potential impact of a group facility on respondents' frame of mine and even their willingness to participate, we quote from a letter we once received from a physician who was invited to a cluttered, unattractive and poorly maintained facility:

> When I went to their office, I immediately left. The office was oppressive, depressing, uninspiring and totally unappetizing. I would suggest to you that if you are ever going to do that again, that you see the offices in which the interviews are going to be held.

This distressing situation arose because there was no choice of facility in the community selected for the research. When the only wheel in town may jeopardize the success of the groups, researchers should seriously consider changing locations or renting a hotel room. It is not always possible to scout facilities across the country in advance of using them, but every attempt should be made to learn as much as possible about a facility before arranging to hold groups there. We also request that our moderators fill out a brief survey form on all new or unfamiliar facilities so that experiences can be shared and future errors avoided.

Every group facility has a reception area whose function is to receive, sign in, hold, and sometimes feed the participants prior to the scheduled start of the group. While it is "off-stage," so to speak, it is not without significance. The interaction between participants in the reception area while they wait for the group to begin may provide an observant moderator with clues regarding the sociodynamics that are likely to be encountered in the group. Participants actively engaged in lively discussion will pose different management problems than those who seem intent on avoiding social interaction.

Access to the interviewing or group room from the reception area should be sufficiently far removed from the observation area so that observers and participants can enter and leave without encountering one another. The group interview room should be large enough to accommodate up to 12 participants, the moderator and a moderator's assistant or co-moderator with sufficient space on all sides to permit displays or audio-visual equipment. The most versatile interview rooms also provide kitchen appliances, sinks, and perhaps shelves hidden behind sliding doors or drapes so that in-store product displays can be simulated.

For physical and psychological reasons, participants seem to function best in a room that is slightly cooler than the usual living room, especially because they are in close proximity to strangers. If the room temperature is permitted to edge up toward 74 degrees or higher, participants may become lethargic or uncomfortable to the point of distraction. Physical discomforts of any kind not only make concentration difficult, they also tend to create hostility. Respondents feel (quite justifiably) that they are doing researchers a favor by coming and should be treated hospitably. A separate thermostat control for the interview room avoids wide temperature variations.

A room that is not well insulated from ambient street or office noise can also be distracting. The sounds of the city may interrupt a group conversation, and on more than one evening, a cleaning person with a noisy vacuum cleaner has had to pause until after the completion of the interviews. Noises can prove even more troublesome on an audio tape recording, when the listener's selective attention processes are strained and audio distortions elevate extraneous noises over voice levels. Care should be taken to distance the microphone from fluorescent lights or air exchanges since those nearly imperceptible hums can emerge on the tape as thunderous interference.

"Experts" claim that room color has an effect on mood and we are not inclined to debate this point here. However, since we are aware of no compelling data to suggest that specific colors enhance participant involvement or productivity, it seems prudent to avoid intrusive colors and to opt instead for light and subdued neutral shades. Even a brilliant stark white can appear clinical and emotionally sterile.

In addition, any structural or decorative features of the interview room that might be distracting are best eliminated. For example, handsome and interesting Chinese screens in one interviewing room seemed to rivet the attention of some participants. In another facility, it was a striking skyline view from the windows which diverted the attention of some participants and actually impeded the progress of the group.

Perhaps one of the more interesting variations in group room decor reflects seating arrangements. Interview rooms generally fall into two categories: the "conference room" and the "living room." Each type has its vocal adherents.

The conference-style interview room is furnished with a large conference table and chairs. Those who prefer this businesslike setting argue that the hard-backed chairs encourage greater alertness. In addition, those seated around a table are likely to be physically closer to one another than in the living-room configuration, and this proximity facilitates social interaction. At the same time, leg postures can be ignored, thus eliminating one potential source of discomfort and self-consciousness. Finally, in a conference room, the table serves as a surface upon which stimulus materials can be displayed and paper and pencil tasks completed.

The living room (as its name implies) mimics a cozy, informal home environment, and advocates of this arrangement hold that it fosters a more relaxed, less guarded social climate. However, our own experience does not confirm this. In fact, it seems to us that people seated casually among strangers may actually value the physical protection of a table, which serves as bulwark and body rest for respondents as they ease their way toward interaction. There is also a risk that the very furnishings needed to create a living-room ambience will in themselves be a distraction.

On balance, we prefer the conference room, whose broader appeal seems to be confirmed by the overwhelming prevalence of this style in group rooms across the country. Choice of setting should generally be dictated by features other than room design, particularly the caliber of the recruiting capabilities, the efficiency of the facility, and its location.

With few exceptions, the conference tables in group rooms are rectangular, a likely result of the greater availability of rectangular tables and/or rectangular rooms, rather than any deliberate decision by those designing group rooms. We believe, however, that table shape has some impact on group dynamics and deserves at least passing attention. Some configurations are preferable to others, although none is without some disadvantages.

There are many persuasive arguments to be made in favor of either a round table or a square one. Perhaps the most compelling asset is that participants can be seated so that each has more direct eye contact with all of the others in order to facilitate interaction. Some rectangular tables are so long that discussion between participants at polar ends of the same side of the table is discouraged. When respondents are seated around a circle or square, it is more difficult for passive members of the group to slip off into social isolation.

The round table also invites more equal participation because it is structurally less hierarchical than a rectangular one. One can sit at the head of a rectangular table and the occupant of that seat is traditionally regarded as the leader. Though subtle, the hierarchical implications of the rectangular shape are relevant in the sense that they communicate something potentially undesirable about the moderator's role. When the moderator sits at the head of a rectangular table, participants are likely to expect more active direction and leadership than they might from a moderator seated at any point around a circular table. The round table does not negate or deny the leadership of the moderator—surely King Arthur intended no abdication of leadership at his Round Table—but the circular arrangement better supports the moderator's invitation for everyone to participate. It also dissuades group members from expecting that the moderator will actively direct or govern proceedings by asking questions or providing information.

There is one additional virtue to the round table. Just as participants have better views of one another, so does the moderator have a better perspective from which to observe the group. It is not unusual for a respondent to lean forward over the table to seek the moderator's attention and, by doing so, obscure the moderator's view of other participants. Keen and constant observation is crucial to sound group management; anything that limits the moderator's visual perspective will handicap moderating effectiveness.

The round table is not without its own limitations, however. In order to make eye contact with a respondent seated directly next to the moderator at a round table, it is often necessary for the moderator to crane his or her neck and back away from other respondents. In doing so, the moderator not only loses some control over group interaction by exchanging and manipulating eye contact; he or she also misses facial expressions and unspoken reactions elsewhere in the room. Another shortcoming of the round table is that respondents are often close enough to examine the moderator's materials, and that is generally undesirable.

In response to these concerns, we have seen some attempts in newer facilities to customize group tables with kidney shapes, pie wedges, and other interesting variations. Some of these are more successful than others. A flattened or elongated semicircle in one elegant facility placed respondents in such a way that the moderator could see them all at a glance, unfortunately they could not easily make eye contact with one another. The configuration discouraged interaction and seemed to remind respondents that they were lined up in front of a mirror. Its principal virtue was that it gave the client a broad vantage point from which to observe facial reactions to videotaped material.

What comes closest to the ideal for some moderators is an elliptical or kidney shape that avoids extreme angles and maximizes visibility for everyone. Practical considerations are such that moderators must learn to accommodate themselves to a wide variety of situations and conditions.

The viewing environment Viewing rooms should be large enough to comfortably accommodate up to eight observers, and the mirror should permit a clear view of all participants. In the past, considerable pains were taken to disguise the function of the mirror by integrating it into the decor of the group room. Today, that implicit deception has been abandoned and the moderator routinely announces the function of the mirror at the beginning of each session. It is our firm conviction that the moderator should always sit with his or her back to the mirror so that observers have an unobstructed view of all the respondents. There are a few facilities in which the mirror is placed alongside the table so that half the participants are seated with their back to the observers. We believe that this is entirely unacceptable and while we tolerate many table shapes and room arrangements, we make a point of avoiding that one.

When mirror-equipped group facilities are not available (and this is rare in medium to large cities), the question arises as to how observation may be arranged. Two options are available: (1) provide closed-circuit television transmission to observers in a remote room, or (2) invite the observers into the group room itself.

Some moderators raise strong objections to the presence of observers in the group room, arguing that this is potentially distracting and intrusive. Clearly objectionable are observers who cannot control their responses to what is being said and who convey pleasure or displeasure, amusement or anguish by facial expression or bodily gesture. Even poker-faced observers may be watched attentively for signals, since they are assumed by participants to be clients with a vested interest or stake in the proceedings.

The other alternative—closed-circuit television—has deficiencies of its own. First, observing a group via TV monitor is decidedly less immediate and involving than observing through a mirror or actually sitting in the group room. Electronic mediation seems to impose an emotional as well as physical distance between the observed and the observer.

Second, the view one has of each participant is governed by the perspective of a fixed camera or the skill of a technician, and the presence of technician in the group room may also be initially distracting to participants.

On balance, if observers are properly cautioned and self-controlled, their presence in the group room may pose fewer problems to the moderator than closed-circuit TV generally poses to the observers. Accordingly, our preference is to invite observers into the group room but only after a thorough briefing about the potential impact of their behavior on the group. Needless to say, lapel pins, tie clips, pens, notebooks or attache cases with company insignia should all be discarded before entering the group room if the sponsor is to remain anonymous.

It is best to seat observers at chairs around the room or at a separate table so that they can see the faces of all participants. Rarely has this arrangement seemed to limit the productivity or free-wheeling candor of the session. Groups are stifled only by observers who adopt a gloomy or troubled look when their new product concept is being dismissed contemptuously and exude a rapturous glow when next year's line extension is applauded. Observers who are not emotionally responsive are generally ignored after about the first ten minutes.

RECRUITING PROCEDURES

As already noted, most marketing researchers must rely on professional group facilities to recruit and host the sessions in any given location. Thus, the facility selected will generally determine the caliber and the integrity of the recruiting process. Whoever commissions and designs the study, however, is directly responsible for setting the procedures and specifications.

Determining Whom To Call

While procedures for respondent selection and screening will vary with the group facility, agencies do not necessarily begin with a randomly generated list of individuals. Often, respondents are drawn from a pre-screened pool of people whose names have been gathered informally on a referral basis from prior respondents and other primary contacts known to the recruiting agency. Some organizations with central location facilities may periodically refresh their lists by administering general screeners to passersby or making random telephone calls. Nevertheless, rigorous standards of probability sampling have not traditionally been met in group screening procedures because it was long felt that blind calls would produce unacceptably low response rates (particularly in large northeastern metropolitan areas). In addition, the gain from random calling is hard to measure in qualitative research.

Under pressure from clients, however, some agencies are modifying their recruiting techniques and are having reasonable success with random calls. This probably reflects a growing familiarity and experience with the group interview concept, as well as the heavy traffic patterns in suburban malls where so many facilities are located. However, since there is substantial variation in the response rate obtained in different cities and facilities, clients who wish random calling would do well to heed the prior experience of the agency or be prepared to assume some risk. What is clear is that experienced telephone recruiters and well-supervised calls are needed for random screening, and in some locations even those are not enough to make random recruiting procedures cost efficient.

People who question whether referral or "snowball" techniques diminish the value of group interviews can be reassured unequivocally that they do not. Qualitative research does not aspire to statistical reliability so procedures designed to satisfy probability sampling requirements are largely irrelevant. What researchers should aim for is some reassurance that the people they interview are relevant to the market of interest and have no specific characteristics that would set limits on the value of their participation.

Clients are sometimes able to provide a list of prospective participants drawn from customer lists, mailing lists, directories, or other industry sources. When they do, it is generally wise to require *at least* four names for every respondent needed, unless interest in attending is expected to be unusually high or a special incentive is provided. Even if the interest level is thought to be high, a surplus of names is prudent because, as recruiters know well, lists are always rife with errors and duplications, and often need to be expanded or abandoned. The reassurance that "this is a good list" or "we base our whole business on this list," should *never* be taken as grounds for optimism.

Screening

The instrument for implementing recruiting specifications is the screening form, a brief questionnaire designed to (1) dictate the flow of screening questions, (2) serve as a basis for tracking general incidence (if desired), and (3) provide a record of the responses supplied by those ultimately selected for the groups.

A good screening form follows all of the principles and conventions of good questionnaire design, a subject which falls outside the purview of this book. It is worth noting, however, that unlike ordinary questionnaires which are designed as information-gathering tools, screening forms function *largely as means to an end—such as determining eligibility—and their structure is dictated by that objective.*

For example, it is generally desirable to structure the screening form in such a way that prospective respondents are not alerted to the factors on which eligibility depends. For example, if one wishes to interview frequent readers of a particular magazine, it may be desirable to ask a few additional camouflage questions about magazines unrelated to the object of the group interview.

The value of the comoflage is twofold. First, it discourages respondents from manipulating their answers in order to increase or diminish the likelihood that the will be invited to participate. Second, it makes it difficult for respondents to discern precisely why they have been selected and then over- or underplay their inferred role in the group discussion. That kind of inference (whether correctly or incorrectly drawn) may encourage respondents to manipulate their self-presentation in order to comply with or violate what they believe are the moderator's expectations. In almost any research, the naive respondent is generally the most helpful.

We do, however, provide respondents with some general idea of what they will be discussing as a courtesy, an incentive to participate and a stimulus to thought about the subject matter. In the absence of such information, curiosity can become anxiety and eventually prompt people to refuse the invitation.

ENCOURAGING ATTENDANCE

Cash Incentives

While most consumers who are surveyed at home do not receive premiums, group participants are invariably paid an incentive for their presence in order to compensate for the expense and effort associated with travel to a central location. The "going rate" for a group session will vary by city, group location (including availability of parking facilities), group schedule and, above all, type of respondent and level of recruiting difficulty. Clearly, a business executive or a physician must receive a higher premium for participating than the average consumer because such respondents are accustomed to receiving handsome compensation for their time in other contexts.

When very specialized requirements are imposed on consumer recruiting as when it is necessary to recruit individuals who have recently shopped for a luxury car or who own a home valued at over $300,000, the premium must be made more attractive as an inducement to those few eligible people the recruiters are able to locate. An experienced recruiting facility can provide assistance in setting those incentives. Since local rates differ, it is wise to defer to an experienced and trustworthy agency when setting a budget for premiums.

We should comment briefly that as a matter of convenience, most respondents greatly prefer to be compensated in cash. Remember that respondents have frequently paid a "tariff" to attend the session (for example, babysitting, gas, parking) and where possible, they deserve compensation in kind. Cash premiums also provide additional flexibility when there is a last minute substitution of respondents and a check made out to Mrs. Jones cannot be offered to Mrs. Smith. Respondents may also be compensated with merchandise of comparable value (as long as they are so informed upon invitation), but the researcher should take into account the risk that interest in a "non-negotiable" product may have an unwanted impact on the recruiting procedure and possibly on the outcome of the group itself.

Invitation and Confirmation Procedures

It goes without saying that the consequences of an empty or underfilled group can be costly, especially when the moderator and viewers have come from another city. Every effort must be made to encourage respondents to fulfill their commitment to attend the group.

Under ordinary circumstances, initial recruiting contact is made by telephone. When a respondent is determined to be both eligible and available for a session, he or she is sent a follow-up letter confirming time, location, and general objectives.

When prominent individuals (such as community opinion leaders) are being recruited for a group, it may be desirable to make initial contact by mail in order to introduce and legitimate the sponsoring organization and objectives. That correspondence should be followed promptly by a telephone invitation, and the acceptance should be followed by a confirmation letter.

The rationale for making an initial approach by letter under these circumstances is, above all, because letters offer greater hope of bypassing a protective secretary and actually reaching the prospective respondent. In addition, they extend the opportunity to present invitations in a more detailed and persuasive manner than telephone contact which tends to be harried, especially during business hours, and it may invite prompt dismissal. Letters generally are not interruptive or intrusive, and they are therefore viewed as both more diplomatic and less burdensome.

In addition to receiving confirmation letters, all participants should be telephoned within 24 hours of the session to remind them of the date and time and to reinforce their sense of commitment. It has been our experience that respondents who have been successfully contacted shortly prior to the group generally do come, barring personal or weather emergencies.

SCHEDULING GROUPS

It is wise to schedule groups so that they conflict as little as possible with other responsibilities the participants may have. For example, it is generally preferable to hold afternoon groups from 12:00 PM to 2:00 PM or 1:00 PM to 3:00 PM so that mothers with children can be home to meet them after school. In the evening, groups are customarily scheduled from 5:30 PM to 7:30 PM or 6:00 PM to 8:00 PM and 8:00 PM to 10:00 PM, depending on the type of respondent and location of the facility. While it is desirable for all concerned to have a brief recess between groups for recovery and feedback, that consideration is often outweighed by respondent preferences. Most participants, lay persons and professionals alike, generally prefer to conclude by 10:00 PM and may resist an 8:30 PM invitation.

Obviously, local traffic patterns, group composition, and the practical needs of the moderator and observers must be considered when schedules are set. It is generally advisable to flow with rather than against the stream of people's daily activities when scheduling group interviews in order to maximize attendance and minimize psychological distractions.

REFRESHMENTS

Virtually all participants expect something to eat and drink before or during interviews. Respondents who are invited for a session at 12:00 PM or

6:00 PM should be offered a hot or cold meal as a courtesy and an incentive to participate. The methodological issue that often emerges is when, what, and how much food and drink are appropriate. The issue is not a trivial one; poor judgment here can intrude into the research process.

In general, the goal should be to make participation as convenient as is reasonably possible while safeguarding the group from disruptions. The kind of refreshments offered need not be elaborate. The key criteria are simplicity, broad menu acceptability, serving practicality, and eating convenience. For that reason, we normally prefer to offer a selection of sandwiches and cookies, cold drinks and coffee. Hot meals are not required.

Where the schedule permits, it is desirable to ask participants to arrive a few minutes before the start of the group and to serve refreshments outside the group room in the reception area or elsewhere. Since it is a rare luxury to have sufficient time for all the material on the group agenda, moderators and their clients grow restive waiting for participants to finish a meal.

The rationale for serving and clearing before the session begins is largely to hasten the progress of the group by minimizing distractions. Eating is an activity which tends to discourage or obstruct conversation. Few people can gracefully manage to talk with their mouths full, and the sound of eating will effectively muffle the audio recording. In addition, the passing of plates or the search for condiments may divert attention from the business at hand and the debris from a meal competes for space with stimulus materials.

In all fairness, it should be acknowledged that this viewpoint is not universally shared. Some moderating philosophies hold that food service is psychologically advantageous and that any inconvenience is justified by the pleasant social climate established when people, even strangers, break bread together. Sharing food and beverages makes social barriers more permeable. It is difficult to remain isolated from someone when you are pouring coffee or passing the cream.

Whatever one's philosophical bent, tight scheduling often requires that participants eat during, not prior to, the discussion. At the least, late arrivals should be permitted to bring in their meals, since the hostility of a hungry and resentful participant is more hazardous to a group than the din of eating at the table.

Note that the objections to meal service do not necessarily extend to snacks and unobtrusive finger foods like peanuts and cookies. "Quiet" snacks should be selected in preference to "noisy" ones. Foods that crunch, packages that rustle, or serving utensils that clang are to be avoided.

We now come to the question of whether or not to serve alcoholic beverages. Some moderators favor the use of liquor, beer, or wine but we resist this practice unless the subject of the group is an alcoholic beverage and taste testing is mandatory.

The principal argument for serving alcohol is that it accelerates interaction even more effectively than food and nonalcoholic beverages. Proponents of liquor also argue that it reduces inhibitions and encourages greater candor. While we acknowledge the validity of both arguments, we submit that the liabilities of alcohol in a group setting far exceed its virtues. Several alcoholic drinks consumed over a two-hour period impair intellectual functioning and compromise the value of the drinker's contribution to the group. While we have seen very few participants become dysfunctional, it is not uncommon for the behavior of some to become noticeably altered. Inhibitions may erode, but so too do cognitive abilities, with a resulting decrease in the quality and relevance of participants' responses. In addition, serving liquor may be culturally offensive in some communities or to individual respondents.

The most practical reason of all, however, is the legal liability to which the moderator and his firm are exposed if a participant has an accident while driving home. Broadened social responsibility for the consequences of drunk driving have sensitized everyone to the moral and legal responsibilities attached to such behavior.

In research assignments which include among their goals an evaluation of the taste of an alcoholic beverage, there is no alternative but to serve the product. Under those circumstances, the moderator should observe the obvious caution of (1) limiting consumption (2) obtaining a "hold harmless" agreement from the sponsor, and (3) reviewing his liability insurance with care.

RECORDING ARRANGEMENTS

Audiotape recordings of every session are routine and mandatory, we believe, even if the analyst has been able to view the groups personally and take notes. Anyone responsible for full analysis must have the opportunity to listen again to the session at leisure, especially to the rich and complex sections requiring careful interpretation.

Video recordings are occasionally requested by clients but are not produced routinely because of the incremental cost. They provide some additional information by affording the opportunity to see rather than just hear respondents, and the fee for recording sessions is often far less than the cost of transporting several observers to distant cities. In practice, however, the value of videotape recordings is diluted by technical limitations and by the technician's inevitable control over the selection of visual elements to emphasize or exclude.

Though perhaps dispassionate in the hands of an unbiased technician, the video camera is still not a neutral observer. It focuses attention wherever it is directed and to that extent imposes an unwitting technological bias. It is also less flexible and reactive than the human eye, which can dart quickly between speaker to listener and react to cues and images of interest. Thus, even in the hands of a capable technician, videotaping is not a substitute for live observation, and its limitations should be acknowledged when recording decisions are made.

The quality and reliability of the recordings, whether audio or video, are crucial to the accuracy of the analysis. If the words of the participant are garbled by a poor microphone or distorted by amplifier noise, it places an extraordinary burden on the analyst to recreate what occurred in the group. Fortunately, technical advances in audio and video recording make available a wide variety of high quality equipment that can be installed at relatively modest cost. There is no excuse now for group recordings of low fidelity.

While poor recording equipment is no longer the endemic problem it was, there is still human error to contend with: a tape recorder not turned on, a microphone input jack not securely inserted, a power cord inadvertently pulled out, the wrong button pushed. Duplicate tapes are standard throughout the industry but occasionally both tape sets are struck by the same problem. The implications of lost data need little comment. Few moderating mishaps cause as much anguish and embarrassment. Much of the data may be recalled, but it can never be entirely recaptured.

A rigorous check prior to each group will reduce the likelihood of problems, although no security procedure is guaranteed to veto Murphy's infamous law. In fact, the moderator's precautions may be of little use without direct control over the audio equipment, and this is increasingly the case as audio systems become more sophisticated. At the very least, however, the moderator should personally test the system for proper operation before the group meets to identify problems and permit replacement or repair.

CONDUCTING GROUP DEPTH INTERVIEW STUDIES ABROAD

The increase in international marketing of American products has made it necessary to understand the needs of those who determine the purchase of goods and services in foreign markets. When this research need arises, the marketer has several options.

- If there is a foreign subsidiary or affiliate located on site, they may arrange for a local agency to conduct the assignment.
- The American company can identify and engage a foreign agency to recruit, moderate, analyze and report on the groups.
- Alternatively, a marketer may elect to use a moderator from an American research agency. In this case, the obvious handicap in logistics and perhaps cost may be offset by the product expertise or marketing knowledge of a particular moderator or the comfort of working with a familiar moderator.

If the latter option is exercised, how are the language and cultural barriers to be negotiated and mastered? For a American research agency to conduct group interviews successfully in foreign markets, it must begin with the recognition of the difficulties involved and the problems that must be anticipated. One of the principal problems is the logistics of recruiting the respondents and providing an appropriate facility in which to conduct the group. Unless the American agency has current capacity to perform these functions, they are best delegated to foreign affiliates.

Language is an obvious problem, unless the moderator speaks the language and dialect of the group participants with complete fluency. There is little likelihood, however, that any one agency can provide moderators experienced in a given content area who also speak the requisite foreign language, particularly since the standards of linguistic fluency applied to group moderating should be extremely rigorous. Even the German-speaking moderator who can manage to communicate fluently in Berlin may have great difficulty in Munich. A moderator comfortable with Parisian French may not be at all adequate in Provence. Castilian Spanish will be alien in all parts of South and Central America, just as in the U.S., a Cuban moderator would have difficulty conversing with Puerto Rican respondents.

If a moderator cannot converse fluently with participants in their own language, then a number of options can be considered:

1. *Local foreign moderators can be personally prepared by an American moderator.* If this course is followed, it is the American moderator's obligation to educate the foreign moderator in the objectives of the study and be assured that appropriate methods and procedures will be followed. This may be achieved by personal training visits and also by mock groups in the same topics conducted in the U.S. The latter device is used to illustrate to the foreign moderator the techniques to be used. A competent foreign moderator will be alert to techniques that may be ineffective in his country or those that may violate local convention.

2. *Recruit English-speaking participants.* One potentially serious limitation of seeking out English-speaking natives is that they may be very different from the universe from which they are selected. Another equally serious risk is that English-speaking participants will not speak the language well enough to communicate the subtleties of purchase motivation and image perception. Respondents who are required to speak in a tongue other than their own, particularly in a public forum, may choose to convey simple ideas in preference to more complex ones because they may fear that the more demanding idea exceeds their linguistic ability. Still other English-speaking participants may be reluctant to expose their English in public because of cultural restraints. A group interview with Japanese physicians in Tokyo illustrated the difficulty of using English in a group forum. Although all spoke English, they did so with reticence. They appeared to select words as though they were picking their way through a

minefield. Yet when the moderator conversed individually with these same physicians at dinner following the group, it became quite clear that the reticence exhibited during the group was prompted by something other than lack of facility with the language. Most were indeed quite fluent. It appeared that in the company of their peers they felt constrained by the risk of exposing any linguistic deficiency. Potential loss of face is a cultural onus that must be considered in planning group interviews in the Orient.

3. *Use an interpreter.* The risks of using an interpreter are apparent. First, there is the challenge of locating an interpreter who is equally facile with the languages of both respondent and moderator. Second and equally important, the interpreter must be comfortable with the content of the discussion, particularly if it is technical. An interpreter who must simultaneously translate the comments of Japanese oncologists into English requires not only skill in both languages but also sufficient knowledge of medical and oncologic terminology to avoid distortions or omissions.

Having conducted foreign groups using all of these options, we can suggest no clear preference; the circumstances will dictate the method of choice. In a country where English is spoken widely and well (such as Sweden), one need have little concern about the representativeness of respondents selected on that basis. Similarly, a group of English-speaking European airline executives are likely to be less anomalous than, say, a group of English-speaking television viewers.

Use of an interpreter may be both intrusive and inadequate in a study in which insight into unconscious motivation is sought. While a linguistic intermediary may be acceptable in a study of assessment of a technical product (for example, sewer pipe, television satellites, pharmaceuticals), it may distort or disguise motivational subtleties where they are the principal goal of an investigation. However, even this option is preferable to forcing respondents to communicate in a language with which they are clearly uncomfortable. If the group is to be conducted in English, a courtesy that a moderator may find useful in establishing rapport with foreign group members is to express regrets for not being able to speak their language and acknowledge their possible discomfort in having to use the moderator's tongue.

The difficulties already described focus on language, yet there are a host of problems that may arise as a result of cultural differences between moderator and group respondents. Care must be taken to avoid inadvertently offending group members or giving them a task that violates their own cultural norms. Social constraints are sometimes so fundamental that they can actually vitiate the value of the group interview technique in some cultures. A notable example is in Japan where respondents may find it so difficult to fault a product or to disagree among themselves that they withhold sincere or meaningful comments. Thus, a moderator preparing to conduct foreign groups either in English or in the vernacular, must be acquainted as thoroughly as possible with local social conventions.

Moderator Preparation

Chapter 6

The value of the data produced by group depth interviews is ultimately dependent not only on the moderator's technical skills but equally on the adequacy of the preparation. This chapter addresses the effort that a moderator devotes in preparation for a particular study, rather than his or her general training in group moderating skills or formal educational requirements. Issues of training and education are addressed elsewhere.

FOCUSING THE RESEARCH PROBLEM

The moderator's first and most important preparatory step is to be sure that the objectives are explicitly stated in writing and thoroughly understood. Poorly defined objectives do as much to jeopardize a study as poorly conducted groups. If the objectives have not been conveyed in a sharply focused manner, it is the responsibility of the moderator to assist the client in crystallizing the objectives of the study and then to review them with the client, preferably in writing. This procedure forces both those who are funding and those who are conducting the study to arrive at a mutually understood statement of what objectives are being served. Small misperceptions about what a study is expected to produce may result in monumental failures when the groups are actually conducted.

Some examples will illustrate the risk:

- A moderator repeatedly probed the product *concepts* presented in an artist's renderings of several ads. The client was more interested in the *executional* elements.
- In a study whose ostensible mission was to develop new beverage concepts, it became apparent only midway through the study that rather severe constraints would be placed upon the kind of product(s) ultimately developed. These constraints were dictated by long-term corporate strategic plans and by legal and financial considerations. Concepts that exceeded these strategic, legal and economic boundaries were extremely unlikely ever to be implemented, yet they were probed in several groups because those constraints were not made explicit at the onset.
- In one study dealing with moisturizers, the moderator pursued new skin cleanser concepts that emerged in the group discussion on the assumption that these were part of the study purview. In fact, previous groups of which the moderator was unaware had explicitly addressed cleansing products.
- In another study, a telecommunications product concept was pursued relentlessly by the moderator, without forwarning that the product was likely to violate regulatory constraints.

Explicit agreement on study objectives at the beginning of a study does not preclude researchers from modifying or embellishing them as new information emerges. On the other hand, without a firm foundation from which to launch the research, moderating is likely to be aimless and the results disappointing.

ESTABLISHING THE SCOPE OF THE STUDY

An important part of the goal-setting agenda is agreeing on the scope and bounds of the study, but experience suggests that selecting and excluding areas of inquiry is often as painful a process as sharpening the general objectives. Not long ago, a research analyst submitted to us an exhaustive list of questions for a six-group project that covered 12 single-spaced pages. These were not simple Yes-No questions but rather the kind of issues that require in-depth probing. Each issue demanded deliberate exploration of participants' knowledge, experience, feelings and prejudices. Driven equally by frustration, amusement and curiosity, the moderator estimated the amount of time it would take to cover each issue in sufficient depth to yield insightful information. Conservatively estimated, that agenda would have kept participants and moderator huddled together together for over six hours. A six-hour group interview, if it is well planned and adequately funded, may be within reason, but these particular groups were designed to be standard two-hour sessions.

This is not an isolated example. Indeed, expansive areas of inquiry are the rule rather than the exception in qualitative studies. If an unrealistically ambitious scope of inquiry is attempted, we can expect an unsatisfactory outcome including superficial data, an anxious and frustrated moderator whose performance has been compromised, and just as often, a disappointed client who has sacrificed depth for breadth.

What is it that leads to requests for much more information than can be generated in a meaningful two-hour group interview? If we understand the individual and corporate impulses that prompt these unrealistic requests, we may be better able to anticipate and cope with them. First, the unstructured format of the group interview invites exploitation. It creates the illusion that lack of structure permits limitless flexibility not only with regard to what is covered and how, but also how much.

Second, the value and unique benefits of the group interview are sometimes poorly understood. Despite extensive use of this tool, there are still those who judge the success of a group interview by the quantity rather than the depth and utility of the information generated. The very fact that traditional group interviews are at least twice as long as most structured survey interviews may suggest to some that the number of questions addressed can be similarly multiplied. When that approach is taken, the group interview is almost certain to be misused. Examples are product evaluations which ask participants to "vote" on the placement of refrigerator door handles or oven cavity size, as part of an exhaustive inventory of relatively superficially structured questions.

It is not unduly cynical to observe that an extensive topic outline may be meant to demonstrate to senior marketing management the comprehensiveness of the inquiry and the thoroughness and conscientiousness of the analyst supervising the research. Some corporate market research professionals, especially those just launching their careers, are reluctant to dismiss even marginal issues or to set clear priorities at all. They will insist that the moderator pay token attention even to tangential questions, so no one can suggest that any issue was left unexplored.

Finally, the number of issues to be addressed is often determined by the number of people invited to submit questions. It is a common practice for the client managing the project to solicit research questions from brand managers and other marketing professionals in order to secure project funding and reinforce commitment. The list of questions grows not only with the number of people considered, but also with the variety of disciplines and corporate functions they represent. If only marketing personnel submit questions, the focus of the study will be on marketing issues. If, however, the advertising department exercises an option to suggest areas of inquiry, then there may be questions on what print media are read, what TV shows are watched, or how influential are certain trade journals. R&D may wish to pursue questions related to unfulfilled needs or very detailed assessments of product attributes, and so on.

Since one of the most important advantages of group interviews over other techniques is their depth of analysis, a set of research objectives that discourages intensive probing violates the basic premise of this method. The moderator who attempts to accommodate an overly ambitious topical outline is therefore abdicating his or her professional responsibility. For example, if each of eight participants is allowed to speak on one issue for no more than three minutes, 24 minutes will be required. Even at that rapid-fire rate, not many issues can be fully probed before the two hours are exhausted.

It is the moderator's responsibility to recognize (and resolve) this conflict when it arises. The most effective approach is to enlist the client's aid in assigning priorities to each area of inquiry and then pursue them accordingly. Those issues given the highest priority are to be covered in depth. Others are addressed only if time permits, in an order determined by client priorities. Setting those priorities, however, can create both conceptual discomfort and suspense. Some issues will be abandoned entirely and there is always some risk that observers may disagree with the moderator's on-the-spot decisions about when to puruse or abandon discussions.

The second option is to postpone subordinate issues until some later time, or to divide the research effort into separate studies consisting of fewer groups. Given the same amount of time, it is preferable to explore fewer issues in greater depth (and in fewer groups) than to investigate many issues superficially. Both of these approaches assume a reasonable and flexible client, willing to heed the moderator's assessment of available time and areas of inquiry.

Another more drastic solution is to extend the group. There is, after all, nothing methodologically sacred about the conventional two hours. Participants will often stay longer if they are asked to do so and if they are compensated accordingly. Extended groups are frequently cost inefficient, however, particularly when groups must be scheduled after dinner to accommodate participants with traditional daytime working hours. A pair of two-hour groups can be completed between 6 PM and 10 PM, requiring only one evening. A pair of three-hour groups require two moderator-nights, making a series of groups not only more costly but also more difficult to schedule and complete. Scheduling convenience aside, however, the two-hour limit has evolved (and withstood the pressures of overlong moderator guides) precisely because it is difficult for most people to sustain their concentration any longer than two hours. Breaks and warm-ups will be required after the two-hour mark, and many people may be unable to participate at the same high or introspective level regardless of how eager they are to cooperate.

As a general rule, we recommend that the two-hour convention be retained and that those who commission research rely upon the experience of a competent moderator to guide them in assessing how many topics can be covered in a group session without abusing the technique.

LEARNING THE SUBJECT MATTER

Perhaps most important of all preparatory efforts is learning about the product or service to be explored in the groups. Some studies are relatively easy to prepare for, either because the subject matter falls well within the moderator's daily experience or because it is inherently easy to grasp (like soft drinks or household cleansers). Product familiarity does not always obviate preparation but it certainly makes the job an easier one. At the other extreme are studies addressing arcane topics that are difficult to master and may require an intellectual stretch for the moderator. Examples are studies of computer software, radioimmunoassays, satellite telecommunications or computerized axial tomography.

Inadequate information may result in missed opportunities to probe an issue that is potentially crucial. In a group of oncologists who were discussing their use of anticancer drugs, the following exchange took place:

DOCTOR: With a patient who has prostate cancer I really don't worry too much about side effects. I generally use DES 1 mg.
MODERATOR: Is that the recommended dosage?
DOCTOR: 3 mgs. is generally recommended.
MODERATOR: I don't understand. Why 1 mg.?
DOCTOR: Well, with 3 mgs. you can get long-term toxicity.

The moderator's ability to penetrate the respondent's prescription selection process was dependent on the knowledge that 3 mgs. was the manufacturer's recommended dose. Had the moderator not probed the doctor's use of 1 mg., an opportunity to learn more about the significance of side effects would have been missed.

Just how much must the moderator know in order to successfully lead a group interview on a product or service that is inherently complex? For example, if groups are conducted with radiologists on the design and use of computerized axial tomography (CAT Scanner), is it optimal, or even desirable, to have the group moderated by a professional radiologist who knows as much or perhaps more than the participants? We submit that even if one could find a person with the requisite subject knowledge and moderating skills, such a person would suffer distinct handicaps. In fact, such an individual might not be as successful in achieving the research objectives as someone considerably less knowledgeable about the product.

If it becomes established in the group that the moderator is a professional peer, or even more threatening, an "expert," it is difficult to safeguard the group process against a sort of inversion in which participants assume a learning posture and the moderator slips into the role of teacher. Moreover, a moderator who is seen as professionally knowledgeable cannot readily withhold specific information about the product under discussion or pose seemingly naive questions which another moderator might success-fully raise.

This concern is not merely theoretical. Early in the development of the group interview technique, an explicit attempt was made to train physicians to moderate groups of other physicians on medical topics. At that time, it seemed reasonable to assume that it would be easier to train a physician in group moderating techniques and marketing than to train moderators and marketers in medicine.

The results, however, were consistently poor. If the physician-moderator conveyed, even unintentionally, that he or she knew more about the subject than the participants did, the session was almost invariably transformed from group interview to tutorial. Group members who continually sought, rather than offered, opinions unwittingly derailed the group session by reversing the information flow and physicians standing in as moderators were generally ill equipped to handle the problem.

A second, rather different problem confronted by the moderator-expert is participants' inevitable use of professional jargon in the presence of a colleague who shares their vocabulary. This kind of verbal shorthand can mask subtleties that participants would articulate explicitly for a moderator who is thought to be less knowledgeable about the subject. Moreover, any attempts by the moderator to explore or clarify colleagues' use of terminology (often in pursuit of significant issues) may be seen as insincere and may actually jeopardize his or her hold on the group. A naive moderator has license to ask basic but important questions that might provoke posturing or impatience if asked by an expert.

The third handicap is the risk that some group members will be challenged by the moderator's expertise and respond with disruptive or unproductive behavior. This problem may occur even if the moderator is merely a peer or colleague rather than an acknowledged authority in the field, since the very position as group leader will often give the moderator some leverage and/or imply an "insider's" knowledge not available to other participants. Group members who feel professionally threatened by a moderator with knowledge of the subject matter may withdraw because they fear exposing their ignorance. Although such group members may be similarly reticent in the presence of an authoritative participant, that situation can be salvaged by a skilled moderator. However, if the moderator is seen as an authority, there may be no one left in the group to sanction ignorance. In fact, other participants may react to the implied threat of an authoritative moderator with aggressive intellectual posturing and this can be disruptive if it polarizes the group by forcing other participants to ally with either the moderator or his challenger.

Finally, the knowledgeable moderator cannot help but have personal viewpoints on all or most of the issues, and these views may be pursued by curious participants unwilling to tolerate a noncommital colleague. The moderator without professional training in the area will not be asked to tender opinions. Apparent (relative) ignorance of the subject matter is license to be neutral.

Consider, now, the other extreme: the moderator who is not sufficiently in command of the subject matter. The risks here are equally serious. A primary concern is that the moderator will miss the importance of what is being said because he or she does not recognize its salience. In fact, if either the language or the concepts conveyed are not well understood, they may not even be heard. In one group that focused on an antihypertensive product, physicians referred on several occasions to something called the "B.U.N." and creatinine clearance tests. Because the moderator did not recognize these as tests of kidney function, a fruitful line of inquiry relating to one of the major assets of the product concept was not explored.

The other major risk is that an uninformed or poorly briefed moderator will fail to command the respect of participants and may actually lose control of the group. When group members recognize that the moderator's knowledge of the subject matter is primitive, they may become frustrated in attempting to communicate their thoughts. They may also lose interest in the entire enterprise, interpreting the moderator's lack of sophistication as a reflection on the importance of the session and a negative commentary on their own contribution.

There is obviously a compromise between knowing too much (or rather, exhibiting it) and not knowing enough. In leading professional groups, we find that it is legitimate, even desirable, for the moderator to exhibit limited knowledge so long as he or she appears "educable," and sufficiently in command of the basics so that participants find the occasional task of instruction both manageable and worthwhile, even satisfying. Beyond that, the effort invested in learning the subject matter must be dictated by the needs and complexity of each particular study. Depending on those requirements, the moderator is advised to (1) read selected summary articles in the relevant literature, (2) visit a site at which the product is used, sold or produced, (3) become thoroughly familiar with current advertising themes and positionings of the product and its competitors, (4) understand the structure of the current market (such as penetration, brand share, demographic or regional differences), and (5) know whatever regulatory constraints may apply to claims, product characteristics or pricing.

Perhaps for this reason some moderators have become industry specialists, devoting themselves almost exclusively to conducting group interviews in one relatively narrow market. For example, some specialize in automotive products, others in medical instruments or pharmaceuticals, and others in telecommunications.

There is some risk, of course, that the moderator who specializes in this manner may ultimately become something of an expert and face some of the same handicaps as a moderator drawn from the ranks of the professional group being interviewed. For example, a well-versed medical moderator may come to know more about mechanisms of drug action than the physicians being led in discussion. To flaunt that knowledge invites counterproductive behavior from group members, who may feel even more threatened by an expert from outside their discipline than by a colleague with legitimate grounds for expertise.

But what if the subject matter is so technically complex that even extended study may not equip the moderator to manage a group interview effectively? In that case, two alternatives may be considered. One is to review the choice of research method. Unstructured individual interviews conducted by content area specialists may be a satisfactory option. Individual interviews are easier for a neophyte to handle, and any deficiencies in interviewing skills may be adequately compensated for by content sophistication.

Another approach is to invite an expert to sit in on the group and serve as a resource person for occasions when the discussion exceeds the moderator's level of knowledge. The resource person is identified to all participants as more knowledgeable in the subject area than the moderator. The role of the resource person is carefully limited by providing technical information *to the moderator*. In this way, interchange between the resource person and the group is controlled, and at least some of the problems which arise when the moderator is also a content expert are avoided. Note, however, that if participants are permitted to freely seek information from the resource person, (and vice versa), control of the group is weakened at some risk to the research.

A Theoretical Foundation for Group Interview Techniques

Chapter 7

Before proceeding to a discussion of specific techniques used in group moderating, it is important to make explicit the theoretical foundation on which they rest. Many of those who commission groups are attracted to the technique by the apparent efficiency of interviewing nine individuals at once or by the almost histrionic character of the group as event or performance. The value of the group interview, however, ultimately derives from the temporary social structure that evolves over the course of several hours and the way in which that social structure provokes and facilitates information flow.

The sociodynamics governing group process mirror the principles governing developmental processes in other social, psychological and physical realms. The progression outlined by developmental psychologist Heinz Werner provides a useful model.[1] According to Werner's notion, development initiates in a stage of globality and proceeds through increasing differentiation to culminate in a final stage of hierarchic integration. That basic process is evident in many spheres; it characterizes the progress of living organisms through evolution and ontogeny, the development of

---

[1]H. Werner, *Comparative Psychology of Mental Development* (New York: House of Harper, 1940).

cognitive skills and the development of complex social institutions. In much the same way, it is reflected in the development of a group interview. The stages may be characterized as follows.

STAGE 1: GLOBALITY

When the group first convenes, its members are regarded as an undifferentiated whole by both the moderator and other participants. They are eight to ten individuals arrayed around the table without any social structure to organize personal interaction, much like customers lined up in a store. No one group member is distinguished from any other except by whatever clues are conveyed through dress, appearance or bearing. At this stage, the group is a gathering of people unidentified by individual characteristics or by relationships among one another.

STAGE 2: DIFFERENTIATION

From globality, the process evolves very quickly into an exploration of how each member of the group may be distinguished from the others. Members are encouraged to identify themselves in terms of how they feel about the product or service being discussed; they present themselves as advocates, adversaries, or assume some equivocal posture in between.

Inevitably, differentiation also takes place along variables not directly related to the issues under discussion. Personality differences such as characteristics of ascendance or submissiveness, extroversion or withdrawal, and aggressiveness or timidity also surface as the group emerges. Together, attitude and personality differences provide a foundation upon which the final stage is built.

STAGE 3: HIERARCHIC INTEGRATION

It is only when group members have been differentiated that we see the emergence of a true group—that is, a number of individuals interacting in accordance with some social structure. Ascendant members strive for leadership roles and may present the most forceful arguments for or against the product under discussion. Manipulative members may attempt to present views in less direct, perhaps disruptive ways. Submissive members withhold views, often awaiting the guidance or approval of leaders before taking a stance.

A hierarchically integrated group, having both leaders and followers, advocates and adversaries, mimics the same interactive processes that take place in the broader social environment outside of the group. Indeed, one of the principal values of the group interview is the extent to which it serves as an encapsulated microcosm of the larger social context. Leaders in the group interview are probably also leaders in their own social groups; followers in the group are most likely followers elsewhere.

Thus, we have in the hierarchically organized group interview an environment in which two important events occur. First, the attitudes and feelings of participants are exposed. Second, the social processes by which these attitudes are shaped become manifest and public rather than inferred.

For this reason, a moderator must do nothing in managing a group interview that will inhibit the development of hierarchical structure. Normally, opinion leaders will emerge if they are permitted to. Suppressing ascendant behavior may undermine the development of the group and in so doing, suppress potentially important information as well.

As already noted, this premise runs counter to a commonly held view among buyers and practitioners of marketing research that sees the group as a set of simultaneous or sequential interviews in which each participant receives equal time and weight. We take strong exception to this viewpoint. Without hierarchical organization, there would be no real justification for conducting a group interview.

Only when hierarchical integration occurs can we test the strength and the structure of consumer views in a setting that more closely approximates the environment in which people arrive at opinions and make decisions. The restrained impartiality of the individual interview does not normally subject respondent views to so grueling or realistic a test. By contrast, a hierarchically integrated group provides an environment in which candid, often unexpected, disclosures are encouraged by participants' freedom to challenge or support one another.

The following exchange between two specialists in internal medicine illustrates how that can occur. These physicians represent two segments of the market for antihypertensives (drugs that control high blood pressure). One segment can be characterized as *scientists*, the other as *clinicians*. The *scientist* opened the exchange with a six-minute statement of the need for precise laboratory tests before deciding to prescribe a particular class of drug known as beta blockers for a cardiac patient. The *clinician* responded by rejecting tests in favor of clinical judgment.

CLINICIAN: I can't take everything that Dr. _____says as gospel truth. You can tell clinically—without a 2D echo, without knowing their ejection fraction, [laboratory tests of cardiac function] without all those tests. You can tell by examining a patient if they've got a good cardiac reserve or not.

SCIENTIST: You can? How do you know if someone has a decreased ejection fraction?

CLINICIAN: By their history.

SCIENTIST: By their history of what? Shortness of breath and exertion?

CLINICIAN: By their history, by their exercise tolerance. Have they had coronaries [heart attacks]? Do they get short of breath? What I'm saying is, clinically you can tell if a person will be able to handle a beta blocker or not and not have to worry about congestive heart failure.

SCIENTIST: I respectfully disagree with that, sir. I'd like you to show me some data to support that.

CLINICIAN: You're still practicing medicine in the halls of the university, not out in the field.

SCIENTIST: No, I've been out in the field for nine years, sir. The question is: Are you going to be scientific in your approach to the patient or are you just going to look at the patient, make a judgment based on what you think is the best drug, and the prescribe the medication. It depends on how you practice medicine. How do you pick a drug for a particular patient? The answer to that question is, you get the data to support what drug you're going to pick, and that's how you do it. You don't just eyeball the patient.

In this example, the interaction between the two participants makes their respective clinical orientations toward the use of these drugs very clear. At the same time, it conveys the conviction with which they cling to these positions. Parenthetically, it also illustrates some implicit professional animosity between members of each market segment. The very vigor and clarity with which these views emerged inclines other group participants to array themselves conceptually in relation to these positions and the physicians that most emphatically present them. This social organization, though extant for only two hours, mimics the marketplace.

In this next exchange between two respondents, both of whom presented themselves as nutrition conscious, important differences in their respective positions were clarified and sharpened through adversarial dialogue. A respondent, labeled here "nutrition-conscious," began her early remarks in the group by attempting to establish herself as a nutrition authority in active pursuit of health foods. It was only in response to the more extreme position taken by another respondent, referred to here as the "health food advocate," that the limits of her commitment and zeal were more clearly drawn. The two participants reflect discrete market segments which, despite some convergence of values and behaviors, should be distinguished carefully for marketing purposes.

NUTRITION-CONSCIOUS: I would have to say I'm a lot more concerned than I was a few years ago about what goes into my body. I try to stay away from salt, preservatives, things that I believe are bad for you ... I'm eating a lot more cheese instead of red meat. And I'm really careful about reading labels.

HEALTH FOOD ADVOCATE: Do you know that cheese is extremely high in salt?

NUTRITION-CONSCIOUS: No, I never thought about it.

HEALTH FOOD ADVOCATE: It's almost impossible to find things in the supermarket that are really healthy. Everything has chemicals. Salt. Gums. Refined sugars. If you really want to eat healthy, you have to shop at health food stores. Otherwise, you're buying whole wheat bread with food coloring and that kind of thing. I can really tell the difference when I put that kind of stuff in my system. My energy level goes way down.

NUTRITION-CONSCIOUS: Well, I think that if you shop pretty carefully, you can avoid a lot of the bad things. But you can't go crazy. I mean, I try to shop healthy and eat healthy and I read the labels pretty carefully but I can't buy everything for my family at health stores. It's just not that big a deal to me.

There is another benefit derived from the interaction of group members that serial interviewing does not provide. Questions asked by one group member of another are couched in language that is familiar to consumers and purchasers rather than in terms meaningful to the manufacturer. This is especially helpful when a group interview precedes a survey since, as we have noted earlier, a questionnaire phrased in consumer vernaculer (or to relevant professional jargon) will be better understood.

However, having said earlier that opinion leaders will normally emerge in a true group interview and should not be suppressed, we must also emphasize that skilled group moderating requires continuing management of the social structure which evolves. The moderator observes what relationships develop naturally but must never abdicate ultimate authority as arbiter of the group process. Unlike an anthropologist, who attempts to look in on a culture from a nearly invisible vantage point (playing the role of nonparticipant observer), a group moderator must actually exercise authority—must tamper with the group intermittently—to maximize its information value. The chapters describing specific moderating techniques set guidelines for the exercise of that authority.

Participant Roles and Their Impact on Group Dynamics

Chapter 8

The group process implies some hierarchial organization of consistent patterns of interaction determined by the roles participants choose to play. In this chapter, we review some of those roles: those that assist or promote successful group interviews and those which, if poorly managed, can impede or even derail a group.

ROLES

Moderators and experienced observers often note that the byproduct of hierarchical integration is the emergence of recognizable social roles within each group session. Respondents may assume these roles on the basis of their own personality and social position outside the group, often conveying by gesture, comments or choice of seat, what role they intend to play. However, since every group is a newly emerging microcosm in which any two or three individuals may compete for leadership, the dynamics of group process undoubtedly shape the assumption of roles as the session progresses.

The cast of characters described here may not appear in every group, and any one participant may play multiple roles, but the consistency with which many of these roles do emerge is striking.

Leadership Roles

The *surrogate leader* seeks to play a central and authoritative role in the proceedings. This participant is likely to speak out early in a forceful, confident, and unequivocal manner, inviting support for his or her own views and freely challenging the views of others. Such individuals are encountered in every social setting from P.T.A. meetings to cocktail parties. Leaders stand out and command attention in virtually every environment.

The types of individuals we are calling surrogate leaders have a variety of different styles and may, therefore, manifest group leadership in diverse ways. What all surrogate leaders have in common is a willingness to participate energetically, but not disruptively, and a desire to coalesce opinion around their own. Their presence is helpful, not harmful, as long as they reman in check because they stimulate discussion and test the intensity of competing views.

One prominent variation on the leadership theme is the *moderator's ally*, someone who tends to act as surrogate moderator, assuming a leadership role that is more neutral or procedural than substantive and opinionated. For example, such an individual will attempt to protect the moderator from verbal assault by antagonists and will serve as a role model for other group members through conscientious participation. This person will often confront those who are inclined to be disruptive or who challenge the moderator's authority and may often assume the moderator's role more or less explicitly.

For example, if group members are being bombastic in their remarks or straying off into irrelevance, the ally may bring the discussion back to the topic by saying something like: "Let's get back to what we're supposed to be talking about," or "What the moderator wants to know is . . ." The ally will also attempt to curb arrogance or to police hostility with the special latitude a grass-roots leader can claim.

Ascribed Authority Figures

It is not uncommon for group members to ascribe leadership roles to other participants whose experience or status outside the group commands general respect. This role emerges in professional groups, especially among physicians, but also surfaces in consumer groups as, for example, the woman identified as a prolific and competent baker to whom others turn for advice and information. Authority figures should not be confused with group leaders. Although they may be accorded deference, they do not necessarily seek group leadership. Their demeanor may actually be more benevolent than combative or assertive. Nevertheless, the presence of an authority figure in a group can be destructive if others are so intimidated that they withdraw, fearing exposure of their own modest knowledge or the disapproval of the authority.

For example, one of the country's most respected rheumatologists was a participant in a group interview that focused on a new therapy for rheumatoid arthritis. By chance, half the group members had been students of his and all knew about and had been influenced by his research. The impact of the authority figure in this case was inescapable. No one would express views that countered his wisdom or would even acknowledge that their practice varied from his.

This situation poses a serious management problem to the moderator. Such a group can easily deteriorate into a classroom in which professional subordinates seek knowledge and opinion from a respected professor. In another group, the moderator's attempt to obtain specific and concrete information from hospital administrators on how hospitals deal with changes in federal reimbursement policies was frustrated by the presence of one well respected and authoritative participant who both sought and received leadership status. His insistence on talking abstractly and philosophically kept the entire discussion on a lofty plane for nearly two hours, despite the moderator's repeated attempts to bring the conversation back down to administrative reality by probing for actual examples.

The leader excused himself ten minutes before the close of the group to honor a prior commitment. Not only did the tenor of the discussion change abruptly but, in fact, this busy group of administrators stayed an extra 30 minutes to talk on a more prosaic level. Evidently, other participants were so deferential to this participant that they were reluctant to address more practical issues for fear of seeming less thoughtful than their respected colleague. In this instance, not even an experienced moderator could withstand or offset his effect. Researchers should try to avoid recruiting individuals whose experience or reputation demands deference from others, although no amount of vigilance can or should eliminate all variation in experience level and sophistication.

Diversionaries

There are many types of participants whose behavior, whether diffident or assertive, disrupts the progress of the group discussion. Some actively seek to derail or manipulate the session, others do it unwittingly merely by acting on rude or anxious impulses. In all cases, the moderator must work to overcome the barriers and impediments raised by these various behaviors.

The *antagonist* presents a patently critical viewpoint on whatever issue, practice or product is being considered. This adversary view may be presented in a reserved, carefully reasoned manner (as the *rational antagonist*), or at the other extreme, in a challenging, even hostile manner (as the *intimidating antagonist*). The *intimidating antagonist* challenges the moderator's leadership by asking contentious and difficult questions, often beyond the technical expertise of the moderator, or by questioning the very legitimacy of the inquiry or the ethics of the sponsor. It is often the intimidating antagonist who suggests that a positioning statement is deceptive or manipulative, or that a product idea is socially venal.

Unlike the *rational antagonist,* the *intimidating antagonist* uses emotional, value-laden or inflammatory terms to describe the stimulus material and to question the client's motives, product, or marketing techniques. He or she is more likely than others to interrupt other participants with irrelevant comments, or curt rejections (". . . Oh, come on!"), and communicate a negative orientation gesturally by crossing arms on chest or turning away from the moderator. Complaints are frequently couched in general assaults on marketing, advertising or even the group interview itself. While unlikely to galvanize a following, diversionaries do little to advance the group and may pose an intermittent challenge to the moderator's authority or the legitimacy of the undertaking.

In one study of an industrial product, a particularly aggressive intimidating antagonist launched into a global attack on television advertising, although the central focus of the study had nothing to do with either television or advertising.

> Television commercials are insulting, they aim at a very low level of intelligence. The commercial about the brokerage company is really stupid.

The respondent then described in great detail what occurred in the commercial, ridiculing both the actor and the major theme at every opportunity. Since this lengthy diatribe was not germane to the central theme of the group discussion, it seems safe to assume that it represented an attempt at dominance and perhaps a disguised attack on the moderator in the perceived role of a representative of advertisers.

Intimidators may adopt more direct means of expressing antagonism. When the moderator asked a group of small businessmen how they selected their commercial bank, a respondent who had already signaled his intimidating style snapped: "That's none of your business!" In another session, composed of small businessmen, one respondent reacted to an opening question on the size of his business with an antagonistic denial of the moderator's right to raise the issue or pursue any inquiry at all. Rudeness like this is intended to establish the antagonist as independent enough to aggressively challenge the moderator—but at grave risk, it might be added, to the participant's own stature in the group. Strategies for handling such situations in a way that salvages the group and protects the morale of individual participants are discussed in later chapters.

Another type of diversionary who may adopt a leadership posture is the *pontificator*. Such an individual is distinguished not by opposition or support for the concepts presented by the moderator, but rather by the lofty style in which views are expressed: A *pontificator* states opinions in a manner that suggests divine inspiration. The principal distinction between the pontificator and other leadership styles is the directness with which the major points are made. Antagonists, whether rational or intimidating, tend to be forthright and direct in the way they present ideas. By contrast, *pontificators* couch their views in abstractions and vague generalizations that, while alluding to the issues being discussed, do so in a remote, obtuse way that manages to escape direct relevance.

It is common for pontificators to illustrate or support their points of view by citing their experience in some remote place or time. They may continually refer to the way things were done in the "old country" or in their youth, perspectives which generally have little bearing on the issues under discussion and prove tedious for those obliged to listen. When *pontificators* seek leadership, they often fail to achieve it because group members are not sure of the direction in which they are leading and soon grow weary of their meandering and cosmic orientation.

Dominators are very assertive verbally, tend to make long speeches, will be among the first to speak, and state positions with force and conviction. Unlike pontificators, their comments are direct, relevant to the discussion, and may be articulated eloquently. They exhibit little inclination to persuade or lead others, however, and may express a variety of different views throughout the course of the group. Attempted domination of the group seems motivated solely by a compulsion to gratify their egos and assert dominance. Therefore, the goal is vocalization more than communication or persuasion. If unchecked by other group members or the moderator, the dominator will exhaust a disproportionate amount of the time available, allowing little opportunity for others to contribute. Even more destructive is the effect on group morale; frustration with the failure of the moderator to control a dominator will ultimately result in withdrawal, alienation and silence.

The *evasive qualifier* responds to questions that invite generalizaion by insisting that generalization is impossible; life, circumstances, and his or her own sophisticated purview are too complex to permit global generalities. The *evasive qualifier* elevates the statement, "it depends" to the status of a benediction. In one group, for example, a respondent insisted that he could not generalize about his choice of restaurants because the selection depended entirely on mood or impulse. With patient questioning, however, the moderator was able to discern some generalizable patterns that were repeated, (pizza only with friends, for example) revealing a behavior at odds with the respondent's own self-perceptions.

In some cases, qualifiers may simply be avoiding the unaccustomed effort of examining and summarizing their own behavior. Even people who have the same thing for breakfast every day may have to mentally review their past behavior in order to recognize and acknowledge it. In many cases, however, *evasive qualifiers* mean to imply that they are so singularly well informed and contemplative that simple generalizations cannot do justice to the complexity of their decisions. If such a stance becomes contagious, many respondents will similarly dismiss the moderator's questions and goals as oversimplifications, and the moderator will be required to take some corrective action.

Another diversionary, the *whisperer*, frequently chooses to pursue points by engaging others in whispered conversation. While not necessarily motivated by hostility, such behavior can be just as disruptive. Like the small child who talks to classmates during lessons, the whisperer seems totally unaware of the patent rudeness of such behavior and the discomfort aroused in others by enforcing complicity. Such individuals are generally interested in the topic of discussion but are signaling some withdrawal from or rejection of the group process by placing private conversational compulsions over the group agenda.

The Uninvolved

Uninvolved group members pose a special challenge to the moderator. This lack of involvement in the group is expressed in different ways. The most common is silence, often accompanied by body language and facial expressions that generally signal lack of interest in the proceedings. Uninvolved participants will lean back in their chairs and may even push the chair backs from the table. Not infrequently, such members position themselves so that other participants block their view of the moderator. In this way, they literally hide behind others. When the moderator can see them, lack of involvement is communicated by a vacant, glassy stare into space. Eye contact will always be resisted.

Mere silence alone should not be interpreted as alienation or inattentiveness, however. Some relatively silent group members are intensely interested in the discussion. Unlike the uninvolved participant, however, they lean forward in their chairs, looking at each speaker and at the moderator. They do speak in their own time and often contribute significantly, but only after listening to others.

The *passive acquiescent* is one variant of the uninvolved, an individual who is distinguished by feigned interest. These individuals may speak but rarely volunteer anything. When required by the moderator to express a view, they offer only platitudes or vacuous agreement ("Well, I agree with everything that's been said"), ignoring even obvious controversy among other group members.

Passive acquiescence appears to be motivated largely by social or intellectual insecurity. It is often evident in technical and professional group interviews when the topic is intellectually challenging and the group includes several intellectually assertive participants. It can, however, surface even with subjects as commonplace as household cleansers or toothpaste. Insecurities can be triggered by any subject in any setting.

It should be reemphasized that like any typology, this one is designed to highlight some of the more prominent behavior manifestations we see in groups rather than to suggest the presence of a rigid cast of characters in every session. Many individuals may assume more than one role simultaneously, and many respondents—the bit players and the unexceptional yeoman participants—assume none of them. It has been our experience that virtually every group has a leader and almost all groups include at least one participant whose behavior tends to impede rather than assist the process, but many respondents cannot be typecast. They participate at varying levels of involvement and intellectual vigor, posing no special challenge and often producing some of the most useful and important insights.

PARTICIPANT ROLES AND TABLE LOCATION

Those who moderate groups have frequently observed a relationship between the roles that group participants play and the seat positions they choose. While there are probably more exceptions than rules here, with chance undoubtedly playing a significant role in determining where people place themselves, any phenomenon observed by so many moderators deserves at least passing comment. Several full-length articles have already been devoted to the subject.

One of the most notable and most consistent patterns is the tendency of a surrogate leader to take a seat directly facing the moderator. In this way, he or she secures eye contact and claims a physical vantage point normally linked with some authority. The role implications of this seat position at the group interview conference table have a parallel in the seating arrangement at the family dinner table or at a dinner party. In a traditional family, it is common for father to occupy the head of the table and mother to take the position facing him. At a formal dinner, the host and hostess most often take seats facing one another at the ends of a rectangular table, with the guests arrayed between them.

The group member who elects to take the role of the moderator's "right-hand man" (the moderator's ally) will frequently sit to the moderator's immediate right or, if that seat is unavailable, take the seat on the immediate left. Physical proximity to the moderator appears to express a social alliance. The common, though not exclusive, preference for the right-hand seat confirms a positional bias reflected throughout history, with origins as early as biblical times. It was the view of some Talmudic scholars that the most important student took the position to the teacher's right. In fact, Aaron, who was said to have always stood on Moses' right when he addressed the Egyptian pharoah, was the original "right-hand man."

By contrast, many moderators have observed a tendency for antagonists to seat themselves at the moderator's immediate left. At some risk of straining plausibility, it should be noted that while the right-hand side has historically signaled favored status, the left-hand position has always had less positive connotations, reflected in such cliches as "out of left field" or the proverbial "left-handed complement." Whisperers and other disrupters seem to seat themsevles with greater frequency at oblique angles to the moderator (for example, 11 o'clock to the moderator's 6 o'clock) and passive acquiescents tend to locate themselves at either 3 o'clock or 9 o'clock. Since the evidence for this is ultimately anecdotal, however, it is best to view table position as more of an intriguing hypothesis than an empirically validated phenomenon.

Some moderators have gone so far as to suggest that table position may not only reveal role proclivity, it may actually shape it. They argue that if those who enter the room first actively avoid the facing seat, the participant who ultimately takes it (for lack of an alternative) feels somehow compelled to play a more dominant role in the group.[1] The influence of table position is regarded by some as so salient that it can be used by the moderator to manipulate the roles played by group members, for example, by forcing participants to change seats or by removing the confrontational (facing) chair.

In the absence of compelling evidence to support this notion, it seems more reasonable to assume that adult personality traits are too stable to permit even transient alteration on the basis of table position. To expect otherwise defies what we already know about the inertial nature of personality; once established, it is difficult to change even for a brief episode.

If we are to believe, however, that there *is* some relationship between the roles participants play and the table position they choose, what use, if any, may or should be made of this information in group management techniques? The answer is: little, if any. Expectations about seat position, if betrayed, might affect a moderator's handling of the group and ultimately direct its destiny. It is far safer to regard the link between table position and role as a curiosity of group dynamics—the kind of phenomenon that makes group process intriguing without necessarily advancing the management of any particular session. Whether or not "roles" select seats or seats shape "roles," moderators are advised to respond to participants' behavior rather than table position in managing the group, lest they unwittingly assign roles and subvert the natural group process.

[1]S. L. Hollander, "How to Control the 'Alter Leader' in Qualitative Market Research," *Marketing News*, (January 6, 1984), Vol. 18, No. 1, Section 2, p. 18.

Establishing and Maintaining a Productive Group Environment

Chapter 9

One of the moderator's principal responsibilities to provide a conversational environment in which participants feel free to express views with candor and sincerity. The techniques described in this chapter are all designed to achieve that purpose. Most important are the manner in which the moderator communicates expectations in launching the discussion and the way he or she encourages hierarchic integration and controls disruptive behavior.

SETTING A DIRECTION AND AGENDA FOR THE GROUP

In their opening comments, moderators should introduce themselves, call attention to recording devices and one-way mirrors, state the focus and objectives of the discussion, and then encourage rapid differentiation among group participants. There are several key elements to this introduction.

Moderator's Title

Some thought should be given to how the moderators identify themselves since this helps set the tone and the expectations for what is to follow. For example, moderators with advanced degrees who might normally use the title "Doctor" should consider the consequences of using that title in a group interview. Since so many social scientists with doctorates are now serving as moderators, this issue is a particularly relevant one. Doctor Smith may be viewed very differently from simply Bob Smith and may arouse different behaviors. Some group members will be intimidated by the title, others may feel challenged. Many will wonder what the title represents. Is the moderator a physician? A psychologist? An expert in the subject under discussion? This ambiguity is particularly uncomfortable for physicians, who normally view the title of "Doctor" as proprietary and who, in any case, should not be encouraged to assume that the moderator is also a medical practitioner. In general, the fantasies or feelings inspired by a title may intrude into the discussion or prompt disruptive and unwelcome tangents. A moderator who requires the comfort of a title to shore up self-esteem in a group setting is perhaps not well-suited to the job.

Following the rules of conventional etiquette, it is probably safe and sensible for the moderator to give both first and last names, with the expectation that lay respondents will use whichever form of address is suggested by the moderator. Thus, if the moderator uses first names—which is our custom in most nonphysician group interviews—respondents will tend to adopt that same informality. However, if the moderator does use titles—an approach strongly recommended with physicians—participants are still likely to address the moderator by his or her first name, since this professional group is unaccustomed to reciprocity of rank and title. Physicians expect to be addressed "up" by lay people.

Full Disclosure

The Code of Ethics of The Council of American Survey Research Organizations quite appropriately requires that group members be informed about audio or video recording and use of one-way mirrors or closed-circuit TV by observers. To be sure that no group participant misses this announcement, it is advisable to include reference to the one-way mirrors and recording devices on sign-in sheets. In our own facility, we have placed a sign under the mirror that identifies it as such: "This is a one-way mirror. It is used for client observation and staff training." The redundancy is useful when a group member arrives late and the moderator does not wish to interrupt the discussion.

Introducing the Proceedings

The central purpose of the introduction is to describe the purpose of the session, and there should be no lack of clarity about the subject under discussion. An obscure statement of objectives invites an unfocused, meandering discussion that undermines the value of the group. Even the underlying research goals should be identified (without, of course, violating confidences or creating sensitivities) in the interest of crystallizing the discussion and allaying suspicion or second-guessing. If the goal of the research is to evaluate new product concepts against products already available on the market, why not say so to the participants? If the objective is to develop new product or service ideas, why not inform the group? There is little reason to mask such general objectives and a persuasive reason to reveal them.

One of the many ways in which moderators differ from one another is in the amount of time they devote to introductory remarks. One very experienced moderator opens each group by explicitly making each of the following points:

- His name
- The subject under discussion is _____.
- He would like to use participants' first names and would like them to use his first name
- The role that he plans to play as moderator ("... keeping the discussion focused on the topic," etc.)
- Participants are free to speak when they have something to say
- People should not speak at the same time
- The group is being tape recorded
- There is a one-way vision mirror
- There are observers
- They are encouraged to talk to one another and not only address the moderator
- They are encouraged to be candid in their assessments of the concept
- The moderator has not vested interest in the success of the concept per se
- They will not be quoted by name in the report
- The client will remain anonymous

This introduction often takes five minutes or more. Another equally experienced moderator uses some variant of the following introduction:

> Good evening. I'm your moderator. My name is _____. You will notice from the microphones (pointing) that we are recording our discussion tonight and there is (pointing) a one-way mirror. Behind it are some observers. They're there so that they make notes and talk among themselves without getting in our way. Our subject tonight is _____.

The average time required is 40 seconds.

There is really nothing to recommend one approach over another, since neither approach facilitates nor handicaps the ensuing discussion. Our principal objection to a long introduction is the time it takes. The 120 minutes normally allocated to a typical group interview are a precious commodity that should not be squandered on anything that does not further the research objectives. The information covered in the longer introduction outlined previously is not irrelevant, but we submit that much of it can be communicated nonverbally by what the moderator does rather than by what is said.

For example, the moderator encourages free and active discussion with attentive facial expression and alert body posture. Physical gestures communicate interest when a participant makes a noteworthy comment. The moderator encourages candor by not interrupting people and by avoiding looks of displeasure, censure or shock when something critical, unpopular or socially unacceptable is said. Accepting and attentive behavior speaks more eloquently and more convincingly than any verbal instruction to be candid. In addition, the admonition not to speak at the same time is best delivered when it happens, rather than in advance, since it may actually create undue self-consciousness or inhibit the free flow of speech.

The quickest way to resolve any early social anxiety within the group is to provide the most succinct statement of introductory issues and then get on with the group session by posing the first question. While the longer introduction may comfort some group members by providing structure, it may also signal some of the moderator's tentativeness and discomfort to the group, and paradoxically, may give rise to some social tension. Lengthy overtures serve the moderator's (rather than the group's) emotional needs by easing him or her into the role and "gaining time," but those personal needs are being indulged at the expense of discussion time.

While most participants readily accept both the concept of groups and the prospect that they be observed as well as recorded, some individuals express curiosity or anxiety by asking questions about who is sponsoring the groups, who will listen to the tapes, what will happen to them afterward, and so on. All of the questions should be addressed politely and concisely. For example, the moderator might say:

> I would rather not divulge the company for whom this study is being done because that knowledge may influence what you say. The audio tapes will be analyzed by me (or by staff members) and will be available to our client so that they, too, can be reminded of what was said. No use will be made of the tapes other than for research purposes.

If this does not satisfy the group member and he continues to pursue the point, the moderator may use humor to reduce whatever anxiety is prompting the inquiry (for example, "I promise you will not appear on television, whether you want to or not!"). In using humor, however, the moderator must always remain sensitive to the disarming and intimidating impact that jokes may have on insecure participants, since egos must never be injured by the group experience.

Initiating Discussion

The task of encouraging rapid group differentiation and interaction is best accomplished by inviting (or forcing, if necessary) each group member to contribute something *related to the focus of discussion* as early in the session as possible. This principle runs counter to a commonly followed warm-up procedure which asks for personal introductions about employment status, family configuration, and so on. There is disagreement on how truly useful this brief phase may actually be. In selecting moderating strategies, moderators are advised to consider carefully whether the personal information elicited in this way actually accelerates group interaction and/or is useful to them and observers insofar as it may uncover problems of eligibility or signal relevant characteristics that set a context for the interpretation of later remarks.

To facilitate the group process, initial substantive questions can be posed to the group as a whole, without personal preliminaries. Ideally, the question should be a provocative one that invites reflection rather than a simple "Yes" or "No." Questions like "What is the role of the pharmacist in recommending over-the-counter drugs?" or "How have your eating goals and habits been changing in the last year?" are ego involving and invite participants to reflect on their own behaviors. Usually, one group member volunteers to begin the discussion. If everyone remains silent and an uncomfortable conservational void develops, the moderator can ease the transition by inviting one group member to comment on the moderator's question. That is usually all that is needed to get the conversation underway.

There is some danger that initially calling on any one participant may set an unfortunate precedent and that other members may continue to wait until they are called upon, creating an undesirable constraint on spontaneity and interaction. However, if the moderator selects the participant who already seems most primed to speak and who requires no more than a gentle nudge to begin comment, little harm is done. A lifted eyebrow, a nodded head, or simply direct eye contact is often all that is needed.

ESTABLISHING A SUPPORTIVE, NON EVALUATIVE CLIMATE

The successful use of all in-depth interviewing techniques requires an ability to listen very attentively to what group members are saying. Skilled listening is a knack that some people acquire naturally but most of us must be trained in the art. In a group session, the moderator's attention is continually fragmented by a need to evaluate the relevance of comments, to direct the discussion toward issues not yet addressed, to monitor the amount of time left, to control disruptive group members, and all the while to concentrate closely on what is being said, not only the words but their meaning and implications.

Attentive listening is, of course, necessary to guide the group skillfully through the areas of inquiry. In addition, it has a salutary effect on the group process because careful, conscientious listening is flattering. It conveys to the speaker that what is being said is worthy of attention. It also provides a role model for group members. The more attentively the moderator listens, the more likely group members are to listen to one another. Thus, the moderator must not only listen but should also *appear* to be listening; he communicates his interest through eye contact, body position, physical gesture, and an appropriate follow-up question or comment. When something particularly relevant is being said, the moderator may lean forward toward the speaker to encourage further comment.

Careful listening also helps the moderator manage a group by pointing out patterns and inconsistencies in their responses. A moderator who catches and stores participants' comments can later recall them to group members by way of contrast with what is being said currently. Few things please group members more than hearing their words recalled later in the group, even if only to point out an inconsistency. Listening and remembering is viewed as a sincere gesture of esteem.

The moderator creates a supportive, nonjudgmental climate not only by appearing to listen intently, but also by carefully controlling his or her facial expression to avoid communicating censure or disapproval while comments are being made. This does not mean to imply that the ideal expression is the classic "poker face" which masks all feelings, positive as well as negative. On the contrary, a relaxed and pleasant manner is very effective in establishing rapport and encouraging respondents to feel comfortable expressing intimate or socially unacceptable sentiments. The moderator who fails to smile or laugh at clearly signaled jokes is communicating distance, discouraging spontaneity and suppressing the natural group process.

It is especially important that the moderator use supportive facial gestures to reinforce ideas which appear to reflect more profound insights, moving the discussion beyond superficial disclosure. An entirely impassive expression can actually communicate to respondents that they have said nothing worthwhile or perhaps that they have said something unacceptable. The moderator's goal is to suggest to others by posture, expression and direct comment that a person who is giving serious thought to the subject and avoiding glib or superficial comments is making an important contribution. However, care should be taken to avoid the implication that a particular viewpoint is somehow correct or superior. This can be achieved by suggesting to the group that the comment was extremely interesting and thought provoking. Might others in the group share it or feel differently on the subject?

ENCOURAGING HIERARCHIC INTEGRATION

We have argued here that the objectives of group depth interviewing can be most effectively met when participants interact in a hierarchically organized manner. Indeed, it is in the very nature of a true group that participants play defined roles with respect to one another. Movie patrons who queue up to buy tickets, for example, cannot be described as a group. The same may be said about a set of participants who answer a moderator's questions in sequence, even when they are together in the same room.

Moderators differ widely regarding the amount of freedom they give group participants and the extent to which they cultivate or promote interaction. Some moderators leave relatively little discretion to the participants regarding when and how they contribute. In a more structured group setting, the moderator will tend to pose questions serially, seldom straying from the sequence of an outline and often calling upon participants to answer specific questions. While interaction is not expressly forbidden, neither is it fostered. The presumption is that interaction is irrelevant to the objectives of the study.

Proponents of this approach argue that while it may appear to be a set of serial interviews, the benefits of group process are still obtained. Participants continue to hear the views of others and they can still be prompted by these views to discover masked or untapped motivations in themselves. At the same time, the moderator does not have to cope with the sociodynamics of the less structured group and the apparent randomness with which issues are addressed.

The theoretical bias reflected in this volume clearly favors the less structured approach to group interviews. In unstructured groups, the participants rather than moderator generally determine who speaks, when, and on what issues. Less structure, however, does not indicate a total lack of structure. Even an interactive group is ultimately under the control of a skilled moderator, and the control mechanisms are many and explicit. It is the moderator's responsibility to set the objectives and raise the general topics to be discussed. It is the participants who set the order of the agenda and, within practical limits set by the moderator, decide the amount of attention given each topic.

Participant differentiation will normally occur without active intervention of a moderator. When eight to ten people are seated at the same table, the sociodynamics of group formation provide for the emergence of individual roles. Leaders and followers, antagonists and advocates, verbally hyperactive and hypoactive group members will all ultimately surface.

One technique used by group therapists to encourage responses from the group is silence. A similar tactic can be used by moderators. Once discussion starts, it is best for the moderator to indicate by silence and body posture that he or she expects the group to continue the conversation with one another on their own. This can be signaled by leaning back in the seat or, to emphasize the point further, pushing the chair back from the table just a bit. Should group discussion quickly subside, the moderator can remain silent. The awkwardness or discomfort of silence motivates some group members to seize leadership or perhaps express anxiety, thus initiating the development of the group process.

If role differentiation is impeded by an especially quiet group or dominated by one member, then it is the responsibility of the moderator to accelerate the process. Verbally active members do not require moderator prompting but the reticent, uninvolved, or acquiescent participants do. How, then, does the moderator encourage participation from the more taciturn members without threatening them or causing social discomfort? A moderator who aggressively demands active participation may risk subjecting members to unnecessary discomfort and may, in fact, achieve a less spontaneous and sustained level of interaction. If the moderator can quickly establish a casual and accepting conversational environment, passive group members may need only a gentle nudge in order to participate.

For truly recalcitrant group members, active intervention may be required in progressively more forceful steps. Engaging sustained eye contact, and if necessary, calling upon specific participants for a comment or reaction will generally encourage at least minimal involvement. Some uninvolved members require frequent prompting to sustain continuing participation and after a series of such attempts, a moderator may well decide to abandon the pursuit. Direct interrogation of the intractably uninvolved does not necessarily advance our understanding of the topic (or the participant's own views on it) and tends to violate the terms or procedures of the group. It often constitutes little more than pro forma "vote counting."

When all of the group members do contribute, whether spontaneously or in response to some direct provocation, differentiation generally occurs quickly, perhaps within the first 15 to 20 minutes. The role that each group member intends to play is communicated to other group members with remarkable efficiency. Progression to the next stage in which members interact with one another in a manner consistent with their roles may require aditional effort. However, if that hierarchic integration does not occur, it is the responsibility of the moderator to promote and acclerate it. Otherwise, a pattern may be established in which each of the group members speak only to the moderator, and mainly in response to the moderator's questions.

Once participant differentiation has occurred, the moderator should avoid asking questions of group members in sequence. Doing so imposes a reactive posture upon the group and implicitly discourages group interaction. A question can be asked of the group as a whole without placing the burden of response on any particular respondent.

Thus, the moderator may ask, "What do you think of this idea?" after presenting a concept statement or a story board, and then await a response from whichever group member elects to answer first. Moderator patience and self-discipline at this point will convey to the group that spontaneous interaction is expected.

Some participants will resist even the most deliberate attempts to foster group interaction, however, and will address the moderator to the apparent exclusion of everyone else in the group. It is often possible to discourage this behavior by manipulating eye contact. While the participant is speaking, the moderator looks steadfastly as someone else in the group, thereby diverting the speaker's attention to some other point (and person) in the room. This maneuver usually works well but it requires the moderator to behave in a manner that is socially uncomfortable. Moderator-trainees find it especially difficult; they cannot abandon the deeply ingrained convention of looking at the person who is speaking. The risk it involves is that the participant who is speaking may actually draw the inference that his comments are inappropriate or unwelcome. Avoiding eye contact is, in fact, one effective method for suppressing an excessively garrulous respondent.

A more blatant tactic for engaging group members in discussion with one another is to explicitly invite a person to comment on a point made by some other participant. For example, if a group member demands the attention of the moderator and appears to exclude the rest of the group, the moderator may ask for comment from a group member who is likely to have the strongest feelings about the point being made. ("John, you seem to have some thoughts about that. What are your feelings about what Harry just said?") Note that the reference to both "thoughts" and "feelings" in this inquiry is deliberate in that it encompasses both rational, cognitive processes as well as a more subjective and emotional response.

The time and effort required to encourage interaction is usually rewarded with group candor and conscientiousness. *There are, however, circumstances under which the pursuit of hierarchic integration should be abandoned.* Notably, if the research agenda is overcrowded and cannot be accommodated in the customary two-hour session, the moderator may have little choice but to abandon the integrated group methodology in favor of a technique that approximates serial individual interviewing. In this procedure, the moderator is far more dominant and intrusive, more likely to ask questions of individual participants, and more apt to invite focused responses. Because much of the interaction is between the moderator and group members, it is best described by the term "dyadic group interview." Its principal advantage over a more interactive group is the sheer quantity of data that is elicited and the number of issues explored in a relatively short period of time. In these groups, however, depth and insight are often sacrificed for breadth, since time restrictions require the moderator to focus on behavior without probing underlying motives. Often such research objectives may be more appropriately addressed by structured quantitative techniques. It is difficult, in our view, to make a truly persuasive argument for this pseudogroup interview approach over a series of individual (or private) depth interviews.

DISCOURAGING UNPRODUCTIVE BEHAVIOR

In the cause of creating a productive group environment, the moderator must strive to control and curtail anything that limits or disrupts the flow of relevant information. This section focuses upon managing participants whose aggressive behavior may disrupt the group or whose very stature and knowledgeability may discourage others from contributing.

Controlling Destructive Domination

In the preceding chapter, we mentioned a number of different roles, some generally positive and supportive of group interaction, and others such as antagonists and dominators which suppress active exchange and sometimes alienate other group members. Particularly troublesome is the dominator whose compulsion to speak may derail conversation and deprive others of the opportunity to contribute. Failure to control the dominator not only results in a loss of productive group time, it may also signal to others the moderator's weak hold on the group, and this may precipitate their withdrawal. Most participants will not struggle to be heard or compete actively with another group member who talks excessively. The moderator should not aim to provide equal floor time for all members but he or she must provide ample opportunity for each member to be heard.

Controlling the dominator first requires that the moderator correctly identify a talkative member as a dominator and distinguish him or her from those talkative and outgoing members who have something valuable to contribute but do not seek to dominate. Some group members contribute much of what they have to say early and then sit back to listen, making only brief infrequent comments later. The moderator must also distinguish the dominator from the authority figure who may appear to dominate by virtue of status in the group but who does nothing to limit the participation of others. Management problems created by dominators and authority figures should be handled differently. How, then, do we identify the dominator? Helpful criteria are the relevance of his or her commentary and the apparent motivation behind it, as well as the length of his or her speech.

Dominators will sometimes not only speak excessively but will also feel compelled to reinterpret what others have said. Following a statement by another participant, one dominator said: "What Jane really said is . . . ," and, in this case, went on to materially alter what Jane actually did say. Control of this behavior requires the moderator to ask Jane if that is indeed what she intended to say. If she is too timid or socially uncomfortable to disagree with the dominator, others in the group may be asked if that is what they understood her to say. In using this tactic, the moderator signals to the dominator and to the group that any one member will not be permitted to control or manipulate the group in this way. Limitations like these are reassuring not only to the group as a whole but often even to the dominator. Oddly enough, it appears that some dominators (like unruly children) look for limits to be set and welcome the imposition of constraints by the moderator.

For the determined dominator who seeks to test the limits of the moderator's patience more assertively, firm control techniques are required. Initially, the moderator can call on someone else to contribute when the dominator signals a wish to speak again. If the dominator is in the midst of a long, marginally relevant commentary, the moderator should interrupt and guide discussion to another participant. ("Mr. Smith, how do *you* feel about it?")

If these control techniques are not effective, the moderator can divert his or her eyes from the dominator or, in the extreme, physically turn away if table position permits. In an extreme situation, the moderator may ultimately have to say to the group as a whole, "I think I understand completely how Jim feels about the issue but I'd like to hear from someone else now." The group is often grateful for that opportunity and at least one person will promptly seize it.

Often the group will come spontaneously to the aid of the moderator who is attempting to control a dominator. In one group, a particularly talkative dominator launched into a very long critique of television advertising when the moderator asked the group for their reactions to a headline presenting a product claim. Most of the vitriol was directed toward the ad campaign for a totally different kind of product and the actor who represented it. Attempts by the moderator to return the discussion to the main topic were unsuccessful. Clearly this dominator was accustomed to center stage.

The group members resolved the situation when some of them allied with the moderator to control the dominator. One said: "Come on now, George, let's get on with it or we'll never get out of here." The moderator's ally added: "It's snowing outside. If we don't move along we may not get home tonight." This was one of many instances in which a group recognized a destructive attempt at domination and acted to curb it.

The intimidating antagonist is also one of the most frequent sources of group disruption, but the moderator must not be took quick to impose a control that would dampen controversy. While disagreement is welcome, any conflict that is designed to intimidate the moderator or other group members is undesirable and should be dampened.

In a discussion of a new drug for coronary disease, a physician carefully described the diagnostic procedures he used to assure himself that the therapy he prescribed was appropriate. When he concluded, another physician said: "You go through a lot of 'Mickey Mouse' that I don't think is necessary and that I don't do."

This remark was made in a hostile manner that was only thinly disguised. The physician to whom it was directed was clearly offended but lacked the interest or confidence to defend his view. The moderator concluded from that lack of response that the offended physician might withdraw from further active discussion to salve his wounded ego. The moderator was thus required to do something in support of the offended physician to avoid losing him for the balance of the group, or worse yet, alienating other group members.

The moderator addressed the group as a whole with the following question: "Do you agree that Dr. Brown's approach to diagnosis is 'Mickey Mouse'?" By explicitly using the offending characterization, the moderator invited both emotional support for Dr. Brown and further commentary on the medical controversy itself. Other physicians accepted the cue and provided both. Dr. Brown, placated by the support of other group members, remained a participating group member.

The importance of group support in controlling intimidators and other disruptive members is crucial. It is equally important that the moderator not preempt the group from interceding on behalf of one of its members by imposing control too early or too assertively. To do so conveys to the group that the moderator does not invite their help and also risks offending the group as a whole. Fortunately, moderator control of intimidating participants is rarely required. Someone in the group will usually provide it before the interchange becomes sufficiently nasty to disrupt the group.

The following excerpt from an exchange between two physicians illustrates how group members will intercede on behalf of an abused member. It also illustrates the unique value of the hierarchically integrated group in which participants interview one another. The discussion in point focused upon the clinical value of culturing for microorganisms to aid in selecting therapy for upper respiratory infection.

INTIMIDATOR: I culture almost all ear and throat infections. Where I trained, the chief of infectious diseases made us do cultures. They did a study on strep infections and he made everybody who came to the emergency room, even for a broken arm, get a culture.

DOCTOR A: What we have to do here, we have to be very specific. A culture may not be necessary. We have to get the age of the patient, I have to get the initital symptomotology, I have to know a little bit about the previous history before the onset of the . . .

INTIMIDATOR: That's all bullshit.

DOCTOR A:	That all makes a difference.
INTIMIDATOR:	You're really bullshitting because . . .
DOCTOR A:	All right, give me a (specific) case, give me a case.
INTIMIDATOR:	If a 14-year-old kid comes in, says I have a sore throat and I just feel like achy and . . .
DOCTOR A:	How long has he been feeling like that?
INTIMIDATOR:	Well like two days.
DOCTOR A:	Two days, he feels achy for two days and has a temperature?
INTIMIDATOR:	No temp.
DOCTOR A:	No temp?
INTIMIDATOR:	Well, 99—100
DOCTOR A:	And I look at his throat and . . .
INTIMIDATOR:	(Interrupting) Let's say it was your kid. What would you do?
DOCTOR A:	You know what I would do? I would watch him, I wouldn't give him the antibiotic. I would watch him longer.
INTIMIDATOR:	So how long would you watch him for?
DOCTOR A:	I would watch him for at least three or four days.
INTIMIDATOR:	All right three to four days to analyze him and he still feels a sore throat. How much longer are you doing to watch him?
DOCTOR A:	Okay . . .
INTIMIDATOR:	(Interrupting) Are you going to give him an antibiotic?
DOCTOR A:	If it looked red to me and there was . . .I would probably put him on an antibiotic.
INTIMIDATOR:	Why, what are you treating?
DOCTOR A:	I'm probably treating a strep throat.
INTIMIDATOR:	But you're guessing.
DOCTOR A:	How often does it happen?
INTIMIDATOR:	But you're guessing aren't you?
DOCTOR A:	I didn't say I don't do cultures.
INTIMIDATOR:	You're guessing; it's a problem.
DOCTOR A:	You're getting me wrong. I didn't say I didn't do cultures. I say I don't do them very often. I don't get that situation too often.
INTIMIDATOR:	The thing is, what I'm trying to say is you can't say 'For you I will (culture) and for you I won't.'
DOCTOR A:	Why not?
INTIMIDATOR:	Well you can't. Because I'll show you clinical studies that say by your eye you're only going to guess right, or see right, about 16 percent of the time.
DOCTOR B:	Don't say what he can say or can't say. He's telling you what he does.
INTIMIDATOR:	But I'm trying to bring out . . .
DOCTOR B:	You may disagree with his method but that's what he does. That's what they're interested in.

Physician B interceded at the point at which Physician A appeared to be retreating in the face of the intimidator's argumentative style. No action by the moderator was required.

When intragroup confrontation is unchecked by other members of the group, the moderator must intercede if the discussion is to progress. The legitimacy of different opinions should be emphasized by the moderator but the fact that limited time does not permit all issues of interest to the group to be fully explored must be clearly stated as well. In another group discussion among women on their use of analgesics, a tactless participant expressed horror at hearing that a fellow group member had undergone a hysterectomy without seeking a second medical opinion.

RESPONDENT A: You're kidding! You mean you let them do something like that without checking to see if it was absolutely necessary? What if you didn't really need it?

RESPONDENT B: (showing embarrassment and distress): Well, I had confidence in my doctor. He's good and he's known me a long time.

RESPONDENT A: I don't care. You shouldn't have undergone surgery without seeing another doctor.

RESPONDENT B: I believe I needed it and . . .

RESPONDENT A: Yes, but . . .

At this point, the moderator was obliged to step in to protect an increasingly anxious participant from a seriously damaging assault, particularly since the discussion was entirely tangential to the main topic of interest.

MODERATOR: I don't think any of us ought to be questioning the wisdom of these decisions. I'm sure Janet felt she had good reason to proceed as she did. Let's turn our attention to another issue . . .

Intercession is also necessary when a group member continually interrupts others. A mild "Let's let Mrs. Jones finish what she's saying" is usually sufficient but if a participant continues to interrupt, a physical gesture such as a raised palm is likely to curb that behavior.

In dealing with an apparent antagonist, the moderator must be extremely careful to retain clinical dispassion and to avoid giving in to feelings of personal vulnerability, hurt or anger. To personalize the conflict is to lose control of the process and perhaps irretrievably jeopardize relations with group members. This can be especially difficult when one participant seems bent on sabotaging the entire proceedings and worse, appears to be having some success. However, even a provocative respondent can be "rehabilitated" with careful handling and may emerge as one of the more informative members of the group.

In a group session on laxatives, a participant sat sullenly back in her corner and responded to all questions with negative or unproductive comments like, "What do you mean?", clearly signaling her rejection of the proceedings. Recognizing the importance of establishing early the right to pursue this sensitive topic and feeling that the respondent might weaken his hold on the group, the moderator struggled to suppress some personal indignation as well as anxiety. He did, however, retain self-control, and without showing outward signs of discomfort, returned patiently to the same participant, politely rephrasing questions as needed. On the fifth try, the respondent literally burst forth with a lengthy account of her own persistent and intractible problems, and she continued to make periodic contributions to the group. Her initial hostility had reflected despair and self-consciousness about her own troublesome condition. Once coaxed from that defensive posture, she emerged as a cooperative and polite participant with important ideas to share.

A moderator who lets a ruffled ego undermine proper handling of respondents may not only lose the uncooperative ones, but may also communicate to the rest a discomfort and intolerance which alienates them all. Ego resilience is not always easy to maintain, and moderators with clinical training have a distinct advantage in that regard.

The whisperer is a particularly irritating source of disruption because the information exchanged in whispers is unavailable to the group as a whole. If the side conversation is brief and not repeated, it can be ignored. If it is sustained or becomes a repetitive pattern, the moderator should put a stop to it.

Initially, the moderator can mention the whisperer's name in the course of the discussion ("As Mr. Jones said earlier . . .") and this may be enough to signal to the whisperer that his attention is required. If the whisperer continues the "sotto voce" conversation, the moderator may rap on the table as one would use a gavel. It is direct and usually effective.

Managing the Authority Figure

The authority figure, though not necessarily seeking group leadership, poses a serious management problem. Group members may be so intimidated that they say very little, fearing to expose their ignorance, or they may use the experience as an opportunity to educate themselves by questioning the authority. Both behaviors frustrate the objectives of the research. Authority figures should be avoided in ordinary groups but since some of them slip through even a careful screening process, strategies must be cultivated for instilling confidence in other group members and encouraging energetic exchange.

If the group seems to be intimidated, the moderator may select one of the group members to role-play devil's advocate. The devil's advocate is urged to find arguments that contradict the views expressed by the authority and to state them as vigorously as possible. This technique gives all participants explicit license to disagree with an authority in a way that ordinary professional interaction might not allow. The exchange can, in fact, be instructive as well as tension-reducing, since the devil's advocate can express ideas without acknowledging them as his or her own.

Managing Exhuberant Interaction

Once the session gets underway, it is common for group participants to burst forth with enthusiasm at certain junctures and for several members to speak simultaneously. While that occurrence is a welcome sign of group interaction and an indication of participants' general involvement, it must be checked diplomatically in order to avoid losing control of the group and missing valuable information. The moderator can simply point to his or her ear or make some other gesture to signal the inability to hear. If the din persists, he or she may need to emphasize interest in all that is said and request that members speak individually. Care must be taken to communicate appreciation of their evident interest and enthusiasm lest the group feel chastened and their lively interaction be dampened or extinguished.

Structuring the Discussion to Maintain Topical Relevance

Chapter 10

A question that frequently arises is: What strategies should the moderator adopt for structuring, sequencing and setting the bounds of a group discussion? While it is certainly true that the group itself will ultimately influence the sequence of topics, the moderator sets outer bounds and selects a starting point for discussion. And, of course, the moderator must never abdicate the right to direct or reroute discussions where they appear not to serve designated goals. This chapter reviews alternative strategies for setting and maintaining a group agenda.

STRUCTURING THE DISCUSSION: "TUNNEL" VS. "FUNNEL" APPROACHES

Inevitably, meeting the explicit objectives of a group interview requires some discussion of topics that are related, but not necessarily central, to these objectives. For example, if the major goal of a study is to evaluate alternative positionings of a new low-alcohol beer, a number of other less focal issues may also need exploration such as participants' general pattern of beer consumption, their preferred beer brands, attitudes toward light beer and "near" beer, trial and assessment of current low-alcohol brands, intention to buy them in the future, and perhaps recall of low-alcohol advertising themes. All of this information is certainly relevant to the major study objective and would be helpful in interpreting reactions to the positionings presented.

In initiating the discussion, a moderator has two options. He or she can begin with the broadest topic (beer consumption patterns, for example) and then introduce progressively narrower issues that lead directly to positioning concepts. We call this the *funnel* approach.

The other option is to begin the discussion by immediately presenting the positioning statements and then provoking or permitting discussion on other issues (for example, consumption patterns or general attitudes toward low-alcohol beer) as they seem relevant. This second approach might be described as a *tunnel* strategy. Since both approaches are equally acceptable, the moderator should feel free to select one or the other on the basis of personal preference and the requirements of the situation.

The funnel strategy, for example, generally requires more time to develop than the less predictable but often more efficient tunnel strategy. It should be avoided when the moderator's agenda is too ambitious. Clients, however, frequently appear to prefer the funnel approach because it suggests a more orderly and predictable approach to topics, and observers are better able to satisfy themselves that relevant issues are being covered. Less experienced moderators often prefer the funnel strategy for similar reasons. The tunnel strategy requires greater self-confidence, less rigid attention to the outline, and greater skill in interweaving and transitioning topics that do not necessarily flow in an orderly progression.

DETERMINING RELEVANCE

Regardless of which general strategy the moderator pursues, there is every likelihood that at some point the discussion will veer toward issues which, while not unrelated to the study objectives, are deemed by the moderator to be inactionable or unproductive. This is one of the principal hazards of the conversational nature of the group interview. Unfortunately, dalliance on irrelevant or ancillary topics competes for the limited time available to explore more crucial ones. The moderator who allows the discussion to stray aimlessly is abdicating a major responsibility.

In maintaining relevance, the moderator faces two simultaneous challenges. The first is to assess whether the issues being discussed are relevant. The second is to direct group participants toward relevant material without intimidating or alienating them.

The true relevance of a discussion to the study objectives is not always immediately apparent to the moderator or the participant who raised it. In assessing relevance, the moderator must consider (1) how important background information is to the client and (2) whether reactions to the concepts can be interpreted without a thorough understanding of each participant's consumption patterns and general attitudes toward the category.

In the case of the low-alcohol study, information about each participant was necessary in order to understand the motivational foundation upon which his or her reactions to the advertising positionings rested. Similarly, in a study of reactions to new menstrual remedies, a discussion of general attitudes toward drugs, self-medication and even female physiology, was fundamental to our understanding of the way respondents evaluated the new concept. Those who believed that it is inappropriate or unnatural to take medication for menstrual pain were telling us something different about our marketing barriers and opportunities than those who believe menstrual cramps should receive the same kind of attention as a headache.

Often, however, such background material has already been fully explored in prior studies for the same client and contributes little to the research objectives. It is fruitless to pursue material that is not directly relevant to the study of objectives merely to adhere to the apparent logic of the traditonal funnel strategy.

The moderator may conclude that an exchange which appears superficially relevant may actually be tangential in the sense that no actionable conclusions can arise from it. In a group discussion with food authorities on eating trends, the moderator was obliged to terminate a discussion on whether American foods are less nutritious than European foods, since no marketing guidance would emerge from that exchange and the agenda was already a busy one.

Making these judgments promptly and correctly requires that the moderator thoroughly appreciate the study goals. In another case of a group session whose focus was on attitudes toward baking from "scratch" and preference for cake flour brands, one woman made a casual comment about suspending baking when she was pregnant. The comment elicited an interested response from several other participants. This topic was clearly related to the subject under discussion but was it actually worth pursuing?

Had the study been structured to serve advertising goals, pregnancy may well have been regarded as relevant. A fetus has often been related symbolically to a cake "in the oven," and the powerful visual imagery of a cake rising has been used effectively in television to communicate the creative process of cake baking. In this case, however, the project focused on the intrinsic properties of cake flour and on product improvement opportunities rather than the development of an advertising strategy or its execution. Therefore, the moderator appropriately chose to redirect the discussion.

When the moderator is in any doubt about the relevance of a topic that has been raised, it is wiser to absorb some loss of time and risk an irrelevant excursion than to choke off a potentially useful discussion prematurely. That investment of time may pay off in a marketing insight that only gradually unfolds to reveal itself as both relevant and useful. This following example serves to illustrate the point.

The objective of the study was to develop promotional strategies that a pharmaceutical company could employ in selling to both chain and independent pharmacists. The pharmacists were invited to discuss their reactions to promotional and pricing strategies and to suggest ideas of their own. The discussion developed slowly. Few volunteered. The cool reserve of the group members was almost palpable.

At about the 30-minute mark, one pharmacist responded to a question from the moderator about a particular promotional idea with a seemingly unrelated complaint about the inadequacy of participant incentives. The more he talked about it, the angrier he became:

> Do you know what a pharmacist's time is worth? What you're giving us is paltry—an insult. I'll bet you pay other professionals more than we get. Somehow everyone feels free to exploit the pharmacist.

The moderator's first impulse was to close off this avenue of discussion as patently irrelevant. After all, the pharmacist had accepted the offer of the incentive. If he felt it was inadequate, why had he come to the group? Several options—for example, requesting that he return to the discussion, suggesting that he should feel free to leave, or turning to another participant to continue the discussion—all suggested themselves. However, in view of the sulky resistance manifested by all group members, none of these courses of action seemed entirely appropriate.

The moderator surmised that the angry pharmacist was expressing something of unstated importance to the group and that unless this masked issue was admitted to the agenda, very little of value would be accomplished. Was the feeling being expressed relevant in some obscure way to promoting pharmaceutical products to pharmacies? Intellectual curiosity overcame impatience, and the moderator invited further comment by acknowledging the feelings being expressed. ("You seem very angry!") This invitation triggered an extensive diatribe that focused largely upon the current role of the pharmacist in the health care community.

- The pharmacist is not respected by the physician, despite superior knowledge of pharmacology.
- The pharmacist is exploited by customers who seek advice about pharmaceutical products yet shop around for the lowest price from competitors.
- The pharmacist is forced to compete with discount drug stores, which offer prescription drugs at prices lower than the independent pharmacist pays for them wholesale.
- The pharmacist has been abandoned by the pharmaceutical companies who have opted to address the needs of mass marketers, especially supermarkets, rather than those of independent pharmacies.

- The pharmacist is forced to stock alarm clocks, cosmetics, novels, garden hoses and all manner of nonpharmaceutical merchandise to earn a living.

To the respondent who first voiced his displeasure, the current role of the independent pharmacist was clearly an unhappy and stressful one. However, the general support given the speaker made it clear that this view was shared by most of the others. This was not the complaint of a professional isolate and neither was it a trivial or irrelevant one. To have prevented the expression of these deep-seated feelings would have deprived the moderator and client of information that ultimately may lead to the development of relevant promotional programs. Companies which grasp the ambiguity and diminished status of the pharmacists' role and provide explicit support for their professional self-esteem (for example, by encouraging the public to solicit their advice) have, in fact, earned their allegiance.

While the moderator must rule on the admissibility of the issues into the discussion, careful note should be made of the order in which topics are raised or addressed by participants, since the sequence of issues is a primary clue to their importance. Points raised early by group participants and those that inspire long, intense discussions often have greater claim on the attention of participants than those that emerge later. Therefore, the moderator should not be hasty in dismissing or terminating them, even if they at first appear to have a lower priority in the research agenda.

For example, in a study of reactions to the imminent launch of a new antiinflammatory drug, physicians ignored the side effects and convenient dosage form that were prominently presented in the concept statement. They proceeded directly to a subsidiary issue: possible retardation of the disease process. It required little interpretational facility to recognize that this latter attribute most quickly generated interest in the new product and the moderator quickly shifted the focus to accommodate the group's priorities. On the other hand, participants who insist on discussing issues that the manufacturer cannot address, at the expense of other more actionable topics, may need some redirection.

REDIRECTING THE DISCUSSION

In most cases, a discussion that drifts into irrelevance can be successfully reoriented with an explicit suggestion from the moderator: "Let's get back to our discussion of . . ." Most participants accept the leadership of the moderator in establishing the agenda. Occasionally, however, a group member seems obsessively committed to a topic that is not relevant to the goals of a study and ignores or resists efforts to redirect the discussion.

Respondents who are politically or emotionally affiliated with a particular view may use the group setting as a platform from which to per-

suade or proselytize others. Ardent feminists, unionists, fiscal conserva-
tives, or ideologues of some other persuasion may seize any opportunity to
interpret the topic of discussion in accordance with their special perspective. The moderator must do whatever is possible to avoid irrelevant doctri-
nal excursions but, of course, must never dismiss meaningful contributions
that are made by an ideologue or a dogmatist.

It is equally difficult to cope with pontificators who insist on derailing
the discussion by reminiscing about personal experience, or dominators
bent on revealing the self-defined and unassailable "truth." If the offending participants are unresponsive to gentle urging, some more deliberate
action is required to avoid wasting precious time or losing control of the
group. This must, of course, be accomplished without offending either the
group member that is leading the others astray or the group as a whole, for
example:

MODERATOR: Let me ask that we suspend this discussion, at least for the mo-
            ment. I have a few other questions I'd like to ask.
            (or)
            This has been interesting but I'm afraid we need to address
            some other issues before we adjourn. I'd like to ask some of the
            rest of you about . . .

By raising a new question and deliberately addressing it to others, the
moderator is clearly signaling both an interest in shifting the focus and a
desire to hear from other participants.

A heavy-handed, authoritarian approach runs the risk of alienating
not only the problem participant but others as well. A moderating style that
is too directive may force some group members, particularly submissive
ones, into silence as a response to the perceived threat of authority. Others
may be provoked into anger or hostility.

If the moderator has been successful in establishing rapport with the
group, a moderator ally may aid in managing errant members. A classic
illustration of this was seen in one group interview in which a physician
persisted in entertaining the others with anecdotes of how things were
done in Latvia when he was in practice there. After the moderator's repeated attempts to discourage these irrelevant reminiscences failed, an ally
sitting next to him gently put his hand on the doctor's arm and said:
"Doctor, he's (nodding at the moderator) trying to get us to talk about
surgical intruments . . . today!" Relevance was restored without alienating
any of the group members or squandering any of the moderator's authority unwisely.

Some participants, espcially pontificators, may insist upon playing the
role of marketing consultants rather than the role that they were invited to
play—consumers or product decision makers. Thus, it is not uncommon

for participants to react to a new product concept by suggesting something like "It will sell to older people who live alone." When the same consumers are asked whether they personally would buy it, they respond negatively and proceed to explain in detail why others would.

Professionals are especially apt to misperceive their role as marketing consultants rather than purchasers or end users but when group members are permitted to evaluate concepts from the perspective of the consultant, it diminishes their value as respondents. Far more relevant are their personal thoughts and feelings, not second-hand observations or guesses about what others *might* do. Group members' attention can be refocused on their own feelings and behavior if the moderator specifically requests that they express their own views. Even dedicated pontificators will acknowledge the moderator's prerogatives, when pressed.

Questioning Strategies: The Role of Probing

Chapter 11

The aspect of moderating which is the most important and challenging of all is exploring how participants think and feel about the products or services being studied. The ability to probe for a profound understanding of why people buy certain products and reject others may be the single most significant criterion of moderator evaluation.

What and how the moderator chooses to probe is, of course, dependent upon the specific objectives of research. Most studies, however, require close attention to each of the following general issues:

1. how decision makers conceptualize markets
2. the factors (conscious and unconscious) that determine brand or product selection
3. how (as well as how strongly) participants feel about concepts or products

While an understanding of why people do what they do often requires sensitive, penetrating probing, it would be a mistake to assume that all useful or meaningful responses are subterranean and difficult to elicit. Product motivations that are easily recognized and verbalized by group participants are no less relevant or valuable for their accessibility. For example, the fact that respondents promptly cite price as a purchase consideration should not automatically cause us to dismiss their observations;

sometimes there are both truth and significance in the obvious, however much we as researchers may be tempted to mistrust it.

Even more profound attitudes may eventually surface without active moderator intervention. The support provided by the group process and by an accepting, nonevaluative moderator often permits participants to recognize and acknowledge feelings that they had earlier denied. A case in point is one car owner who initially ridiculed the idea of buying a luxury automobile to attain prestige, yet later acknowledged the pleasure he took in showing off a luxury automobile to his friends. Excerpts of that discussion illustrate the process.*

(At 20 minutes into the group)

HERBERT: I wanted to buy a Mercedes, I never owned a Cadillac because I think it's ostentatious and I wouldn't buy a Mercedes for the same reason. So I bought the Audi.

MODERATOR: Cadillac and Mercedes . . .?

HERBERT: Well, whoever owned a Cadillac, in my mind, switched over to a Mercedes because a Mercedes was a prestige car and they wanted something to pull into the country club or the tennis courts and, you know, here comes so-and-so in his Mercedes. That's the way I feel about it. And, in the last few years, I think a lot of people, average people, are buying them for investment because of their return.

MODERATOR: Return?

HERBERT: Well, I mean you can buy a Mercedes for $30,000 and use it for a couple of years and still get your high 20's for it.

(At one hour 40 minutes)

HERBERT: I would try to buy a Mercedes for about half the price. Maybe the dealer's demonstrator or the end of the model year. And I figure for about $30,000, I would consider it very seriously.

MODERATOR: Would you really?

HERBERT: I don't know much about it. But I will put my pride in my pocket and be ostentatious and drive it around. (Laughter from group)

MODERATOR: Isn't that a change from what you said at the beginning of our discussion?

HERBERT: (Smiles) That's fickle. I'm really fickle.

MODERATOR: That really is a change from the view you expressed earlier.

HERBERT: Well, for the simple reason that it's impossible to buy a pie in the sky. Right? So why not go whole hog. I would buy a Mercedes. That would be the only Mercedes I would buy, and I would buy it not because of the price only. Yes, I'll go and I'll drive it around and whatever I do, I'll park it in front of the country club . . . and as a matter of fact, I'll call my friends and say, 'Look at what I bought.'

*Quoted with permission of Mercedes-Benz of North America, Inc.

In this instance, the group process itself provoked revelations and admissions that direct probes from the moderator might not have elicited as well. The moderator cannot, however, rely entirely on respondents to express all of their feelings and attitudes unaided. It is the job of a group leader to actively assist in the process without, of course, allowing probing questions to exceed the bounds of diplomacy, psychological tolerance, and market research value.

PROBING FOR CLARIFICATION

Deliberate probing for clarification is required when participants' attitudes are not fully formed or they insist on providing trite and superficial responses. If the moderators are not satisfied that they fully understand a participant's opinion, their principal responsibility is to probe until it is clear, or at least as clear as the participant can make it. Moderators can request clarification by saying, "I don't understand" or if a thought seems only partially formed, "We'd like to hear more about that." Often a quizzical look will suffice as a probe for elaboration. Where the respondents need help in order to recognize and acknowledge their own views, however, more deliberate strategies are required.

One example that comes to mind involved a group of women engaged in a discussion of countertop ovens. All of the women lived alone, yet several insisted that they would never buy a countertop oven too small to cook a turkey. In this case, it was not sufficient merely to ask them how often they cook turkeys (rarely, if ever, as it turned out) because that fact alone did not seem to shake them from their contention that an oven must accommodate a turkey to be useful. It was necessary to pursue the contradiction more aggressively in order to uncover its true significance.

MODERATOR: I want to raise a question about something that, quite frankly, has me puzzled. You understand I'm not trying to persuade you to buy anything here. But several of you said you almost never cook turkeys, and yet you require that this oven cavity be big enough to cook a turkey. Why?

RESPONDENT #1: Well, you never know. My family might come to me for the holidays.

RESPONDENT #2: It's true. I haven't cooked a turkey in two years.

RESPONDENT #3: I want that flexibility, though.

MODERATOR: Well, here's another thing that puzzles me. None of you have said you'd get rid of your main oven. Couldn't you use that if you wanted to cook something big, like a turkey?

RESPONDENT #1: Yes, that's true. But I think of this oven as a replacement for my main oven—something I'd use as often as possible to save energy. So it's a less desirable oven if I can't use it for just about everything.

RESPONDENT #2:   Everytime they advertise microwave ovens, you always hear them tell you it's big enough to cook a 9 lb. turkey, so that's what I think of. (OTHERS NOD).

RESPONDENT #2:   I don't know. Maybe the idea of buying an oven that small, where you can't cook family meals makes me feel a little sad, you know.

MODERATOR: Sad?

RESPONDENT #2:   It's a little depressing after all those years of cooking for a family to cook only for yourself.

This line of discussion, which was more fully developed in the actual group, yielded several hypotheses. First, it appeared that when considering ovens in excess of $150, these women were inclined to demand full cooking function, not just support for their main oven. The issue, therefore, was not so much what they actually *needed* in a second oven but what they felt was their due. It also became clear that the industry itself, in using "big enough for a 9 lb. turkey" as a standard of adequacy in advertising ovens, had actually educated consumers to require it, regardless of actual need.

Finally, there were indications that a smaller, albeit adequate, oven was emerging as a gloomy symbol of their status as widows and empty nesters without nurturing responsibilities. In fact, these women seldom had cause to cook a large family meal; the client's oven was painful affirmation of their limited needs.

It was necessary for the moderator to be directive in eliciting and testing these ideas because none of the respondents were able or prepared to challenge one another on this subtle and emotionally threatening point. Experience suggests that a moderator should be especially alert to motivational platitudes, although they often have some validity, and should explore these carefully before accepting them at face value. Indeed, some of the ideas expressed in a group are so axiomatic and so deeply held that only determined, assertive probing can expose how participants really behave and why.

In a discussion of antibiotics, one physician forcefully expressed the view that cost to the patient was a crucial determinant of his product choice. Every attempt to explore the contribution of other factors was rebuked by an adamant restatement of his concern about the cost of pharmaceuticals in general, and the cost of antibiotics in particular. After he described the cost of one recently introduced antibiotic as "outrageous," the moderator asked what it actually cost. Direct probing revealed that the respondent was unaware of even the general magnitude of its costs to the patient or to the hospital.

The discrepancy between what this group member said and his lack of relevant knowledge suggests that he was ventilating a general irritation about the cost of drugs and using the group as a platform to present his complaint. The physician was not necessarily dissembling; he did not fully understand the role of cost in his actual prescription practices. It became apparent, however, that since he had so little knowledge of the actual cost of antibiotics and only scanty appreciation of even the relative cost of individual drugs, the physician was making specific drug selections based on factors other than cost. In this case, the moderator was obliged to expose the extent to which a stated opinion conflicted with what was implemented in prescription behavior.

In yet another study, a respondent who talked firmly and convincingly about her aversion to using medicines of any kind was questioned about the last few times she had experienced pain and how she had handled it. On each successive occasion, she had in fact taken aspirin, and it was only by bringing to light her behavior under concrete circumstances that the moderator was able to move beyond stated beliefs to more candid disclosures. Indeed, it became clear that in this respondent's view, aspirin was not like other medicines, and its "exempt" status had important implications for the marketing of analgesics. The fact that people may remain sheltered from their own motivations or behavior is significant, since we must take into account self-perceptions as well as actual behavior when we position products.

PROBING FOR UNCONSCIOUS MOTIVATIONS

Deliberate probing may be necessary to uncover the unconscious motivations of product selection. A moderator need not be an advocate of psychoanalytic theory to accept the notion that purchase behavior may be driven by needs that reside at a level below consciousness. The relevance of unconscious needs has received enough experimental and clinical attention to substantiate its usefulness in understanding brand and product preference and purchase.

Memories that cannot be readily uncovered, even with the aid of recognition, may be said to reside in the unconscious.[1] The unconscious is the locus of memories and needs that have been denied full awareness, often because they represent some threat to psychic harmony and provoke anxiety. These mental events are actively repressed or held at bay by a myriad of self-deceptive defense mechanisms.

The moderator should not assume that because a question regarding motivation is answered promptly and with apparent sincerity, it is necessarily the *only* motivation driving a particular behavior. Behavior may be, and often is, shaped simultaneously by several motives, and each may operate at different levels of consciousness.

[1] S. Freud, *New Introductory Lectures on Psycho-Analysis* (New York, NY: W.W. Norton & Co., 1933).

For example, initial response to questions about motivation are frequently governed by ego-syntonic needs—the desire to think well of oneself and to have others share that perception. When the moderator suspects superficiality or ego-syntonic posturing, he or she is obliged to probe for motives that may reside at more profound levels of consciousness. People are remarkably inventive in contriving (without conscious knowledge) devices to mask laziness, greed, ignorance and other ego-dystonic motives that sometimes propel product selection.

One example that comes promptly to mind is the role of image in product categories whose brands may be virtually indistinguishable on all other dimensions. American premium beers and colas are so similar in taste that most loyalists are hard pressed to identify their own brands in blind tests. When asked, however, to describe their reason for selecting a particular brand, most consumers almost invariably cite taste—in some cases, denying entirely the role of brand image, group affiliation, and other unconscious but often decisive considerations.

The importance of probing for subconscious motivation becomes especially important when a significant question is raised about use or avoidance to which there is no apparent answer, and respondents are themselves unable to account for their behavior. One example involved a beer brand that was losing share in a particular region of the country. Respondents were unable to account for, or in some cases, recognize their own behavior. Careful probing uncovered several contributing factors, including fear of product change after a strike, negative reactions to ethnic ad casting, and more aggressive promotion by a new regional entry—all tending to suggest to beer drinkers that the brand in question was no longer the unassailable market leader.

In another group, the moderator was forced to pursue a long-shot hypothesis about what unconscious factors motivated group members to select one print ad layout over another. In this study, a group of purchasing agents (PA's) collectively and forcefully rejected one of the layouts, yet even aggressive probing by the moderator could not expose what had prompted its dismissal. Responses to the initial probes tended to be superficial and largely irrelevant, (such as "It just looks more appealing"). Since we were interested in developing insights that would guide development of a program of communications, understanding what motivated the preference of purchasing agents was as crucial as their preference itself.

MODERATOR: I'm really perplexed about why you prefer that one. Can you give any clues that would help to explain it?

PA's: (No response. Some shrug their shoulders.)

MODERATOR: (to one PA) Roger, if I visited your home and you allowed me to open the drawer in which you keep your socks, what would I see?

PA #1:   Are you serious?
MODERATOR: Yes. If you don't mind, what would I see?
PA #1:   (Smiles), I arrange them by color. The browns are by them-
            selves, the blue and grey ones the same. The drawers in which I
            keep my clothes are neat. It is something I can control.
MODERATOR: Control?
PA #1:   Yeah. At the job things can get very hectic. Sometimes I'm
            pulled in a hundred directions at once. Sometimes things get
            very chaotic and disorganized. Lots of interruptions. But in my
            home I can organize things the way I want to.
PA #2   (Laughing) You're that way, too! I'm a very orderly person, too.
            My wife sometimes kids me about the way I arrange my clothes
            closet and drawers.
MODERATOR: I wonder if that has anything to do with your feelings about the
            layout.
PA #1:   (Nods head) I agree.
PA #2:   Me too.

The moderator's hunch, in this case, proved fruitful. The rejected ad consisted of a display of products arrayed on the page around the copy, some overlapping others, in what appeared to be a random order. The moderator's hypothesis was that professionals whose work requires extreme attention to detail and who can tolerate the many regulations and guidelines that govern their actions, are likely to be orderly, compulsive personalities who may prefer a more organized layout.

Clearly, if we were unable to gain access to these unconscious motivations, we would be missing some very significant and actionable marketing implications. On the other hand, as market researchers, we must acknowledge certain limitations on our ability (and occasionally, on our right) to pursue unconscious motivations to their deepest levels. The effort to search for unconscious motivations is premised on an assumption that the moderator can actually discern when participants are giving a complete and meaningful account of their feelings, and when their comments actually disguise or skirt deeper motivations. This is, however, often beyond what can reasonably be expected from most moderators in a two-hour group session. If, in fact, motives are hidden deep in the unconscious, they are repressed because of some unacceptable threat to the ego and may not surface, even under the most aggressive probing.

The second limitation is one of applicability. Even when present, unconscious motivations may be idiosyncratic and, therefore, neither generalizable nor actionable. In one study of automobile image, for example, a young woman expressed a very favorable impression of Dodge cars but the moderator could not determine the source of the feeling. It was not based on previous ownership experience since she had never owned a Dodge, nor was it based on any objective assessment or even praise from someone else.

Even she was perplexed about why she thought so highly of the make and looked forward to owning one. Determined probing and free association led ultimately to the memory of a deceased uncle who was loved and respected, and he had always owned Dodge cars. She reminisced about auto trips in her uncle's Dodge with great fondness and it appears that her affection for her uncle was transferred to the make of car. While the discovery of the link between the high regard for Dodge and the memory of her uncle was intellectually rewarding, it is not a revelation with implications for promotion or advertising. On the other hand, nostalgic associations can belong to a collective unconsciousness, and memories or motives that are dismissed as idiosyncratic are occasionally manifestations of a broader phenomenon.

Perhaps the best illustration of a product that has become a consensual symbol is Coca-Cola. Interviews conducted by clinical psychologists following the introduction of the new formulation of Coca-Cola revealed the extent to which the product has become enshrined in the collective unconscious of American consumers.* To many of the respondents, modification of Coca-Cola provoked feelings of anger and grief similar to the initial reactions of those mourning the loss of a loved one. A theme of abandonment and estrangement characterized their complaints. For these individuals, Coca-Cola had become a personal memento or symbol of happy times and any alteration in that beverage was experienced as a personal loss.

In the case of Coca-Cola, its symbolic significance had dramatic marketing implications which could only be understood by exploring the unconscious origin and meaning of brand allegiance. It is the moderator's responsibility to take that prospect into account before abandoning an inquiry into the unconscious, since associations that belong to a collective unconscious are often far reaching in their marketing implications. The moderator is, of course, under a personal and professional obligation to desist when it is clear that continued probing may cause psychological damage to a respondent or may create profound discomfort in the group. *Moderators are required to leave respondents psychologically unharmed even at risk of abandoning a relevant avenue of inquiry.*

One might have concluded in reading these guidelines for probing that the moderator is personally responsible for *all* probing activity. To that extent, the guidelines require some qualification. While the moderator should encourage all respondents to provide detailed and candid information, he or she must also look to other respondents for their assistance in probing: Participants may frame questions or otherwise provoke disclosures from others in the group and may at times be more successful at discovering the motivations of others than the moderator might have been.

*Quoted with permission of The Coca-Cola Company

A mother described her continued use of iodine as an antiseptic despite her acknowledgment that it is painful and smells bad. Determined efforts to explore her apparent devotion to iodine provoked a helpless shrug of her shoulders. She could not provide any clue as to why she continued to use a product with such obvious deficits. The key to exposing the motivational determinants of her commitment was provided by another participant who suggested that her use of iodine may have been determined by the assumption that any antiseptic that hurt that much must be effective. This acknowledgment by another member of the group triggered the insight that the sting of iodine also served as her assurance of its germicidal potency.*

When should the moderator personally ask a follow-up question and when is it better to wait for others in the group to offer comments or questions of their own? New moderators often feel in special need of guidance to direct those spontaneous, moment-by-moment decisions. There is, of course, no standard book of rules to consult since each group exchange requires an individually tailored response. We offer only the most general principle here.

To facilitate group interaction, it is best if the moderator waits for other respondents to react to the comments made by a fellow participant, unless the moderator has not heard or understood what was said. Respondents will then ask follow-up questions of other group members to probe for clarification, or they may simply offer their own contrasting or assenting views. If the moderator continually follows participants' comments with direct probes, group interaction may never ignite.

The moderator must recognize that respondents will not necessarily pursue all relevant points in depth, particularly in the early stages of the group. Therefore, the moderator must periodically interject with questions of his or her own to clarify attitudes and behavior fully. A moderator should initiate probes when he or she is convinced that spontaneous group conversation is unlikely to yield crucial insights without active intervention. For example, when a term or concept is consistently used in ways the moderator does not understand or behavior is described but the motivations are not apparent, a probing question is necessary for clarification.

Even if the conversation has migrated to other topics, the moderator can always choose to return to an issue that has not been probed to full satisfaction by redirecting attention to an earlier topic. Indeed, it is often after abandoning an issue and returning to it again that group members are able to recognize and articulate deep-rooted but elusive feelings.

*Quoted with permission of Burroughs Wellcome Company.

Verbal Probing Techniques

Chapter 12

We have been using the term "probe" to refer to all questioning devices designed to elicit responses that might not surface without guidance and explicit investigation. The moderator's fundamental interviewing tool is clear, carefully framed questions—what we refer to as verbal probes. Verbal probes can be augmented or enhanced by other specialized questioning aids which are discussed in the next chapter. In this chapter, we offer some basic guidelines for constructing questions.

PROBE WITHOUT LEADING

Posing a question so that it actually shapes the response is one of the ways in which a moderator may subconsciously influence study results in the direction of the client's prejudices or his or her own. To avoid leading questions is one of the moderator's principal responsibilities, yet that most basic of all rules is often violated because moderators do not always recognize their questions as leading. New or weary moderators may phrase questions impetuously, seeking shortcuts to closure, for example: "Wouldn't this be an efficient, cost-saving system?" or "But wouldn't you use the product if it were proven to be effective?"

In a study that focused upon the design of aerosol inhalers for hay fever sufferers, a client was especially interested in preference for color. It was hypothesized that color could contribute in some way to compliance with the manufacturer's recommendations: some colors would enhance use, while others would deter it. When a participant, made the comment, "It's a nice looking inhaler," the moderator—primed for the desired response—immediately asked: "You mean the color?" The participant made clear that she was reacting to the inhaler's structural design and not its color, but the moderator had nevertheless raised an issue that might not otherwise have surfaced.

A more neutral question would have been, "What do you mean by 'nice looking'?" Unfortunately, however, such a question may be taken by some individuals as a challenge or implicit criticism—a veiled suggestion that their opinions may be poorly conceived or their communication skills deficient. This is particularly true when respondents are being asked to clarify or expand on what they perceive to be a straightforward, almost self-evident statement (such as "What do you mean, 'Why do I like it?' Because it tastes good!").

For that reason it is often advisable to use less structured, nondirective queries like, "Tastes good?" This psychotherapeutic technique, introduced and popularized by Carl Rogers, picks out the key words or ideas that the moderator wishes to have elaborated but does so without conveying prejudices or expectations. Skill in the use of nondirective questioning is among the most helpful of group depth interviewing techniques. By employing the key word (for example "Good?") as an inquiry, the group member is invited to develop further what he or she was thinking about when using the term without implying that the response was necessarily unclear or poorly organized. Nondirective probing is especially helpful in encouraging participants to clarify vague but often crucial descriptions like "effective," "expensive," or "safe."

For example, in a discussion about the effectiveness of an over-the-counter sedative to induce sleep, elaboration would be required to clarify which *criteria* of effectiveness are important. Does the participant mean that the product induces sleep rapidly or that it provides uninterrupted sleep until morning? When consumers use the term "convenient" in describing an appliance, are they referring to speed, ease of use, accessibility in the kitchen, or something else entirely?

Even less directive than the verbal Rogerian technique is the technique of encouraging elaboration through facial expression. A raised eyebrow is universally recognized as an inquiry but its nonverbal nature makes it quintessentially nondirective. Of course, care must be taken to communicate interest and not surprise, shock or rejection. Moderators who are experienced in performing before an audience have some advantage in using this technique.

KEEP QUESTIONS SIMPLE

Complex questions are more likely to be misunderstood than simple ones, and the answers may therefore be inappropriate or tangential. When a moderator asked one participant in an idea-generation group if he thought that a suggestion made by another group member ". . . deserved development attention," the participant responded with a blank look. A less awkward question might have been: "Would you like to see such a product on the market?"

Moderator trainees are especially likely to ask long, compound questions that test participants' ability to trace circuitous dependent clauses. If a moderator has to take a breath before completing a question, it is probably too long.

BE SPECIFIC

In a group interview where all questioning is ultimately spontaneous, a moderator does not have time to decide how a question is to be asked. Generally, however, the more focused and specific the question, the more likely it is to yield relevant information.

For example, in a study in which a radically innovative technology was used to assist in microsurgical procedures, the major issue was whether surgeons would acquire the equipment. The moderator asked the surgeons, "How interested would you be in this new procedure?" All of the surgeons expressed great interest in it, yet the moderator sensed from the preceding discussion that none of them would actually buy it. The moderator promptly recognized that the wrong question had been asked. The surgeons were fascinated by the technology reflected in the equipment but they had very little need for it. A more specific follow-up question—"How likely are you to buy this equipment?"—produced more relevant information.

BE FLEXIBLE

The group interview is a unique research tool in that it permits more flexibility of inquiry than any other. If one question fails to clarify an issue, the moderator is free to try another approach. It is this characteristic that makes the group interview an ideal technique for developing questionnaires. An awkwardly worded question can be rephrased more than once until the moderator is satisfied that it conveys clearly what is intended, and that it is understood by the group.

DO NOT FORCE A RESPONSE

Sometimes opinions are only partly developed and the group member is ambivalent or undecided. To force adoption of an unequivocal point of view for the conceptual convenience of the moderator is to commandeer the participant's thought processes and distort reality. Vague or ambivalent responses may reflect not so much a lack of candor as a lack of conviction or clarity which prevents a respondent from effectively communicating his or her thoughts to others. Some moderators in their single-minded devotion to a topical outline may attempt to force a participant to choose one of several options presented. If the options are all equally rejected or if they do not fit the way in which the participant conceptualizes the category, forcing a response serves more to muddle than to clarify.

A typical example is the respondents who believe a product is useless or undesirable but who, for the gratification of client viewers, are required to state what they would pay for it *if only* they liked it. That kind of hypothetical or conjectural questioning ("If you had a brother, would he like noodles?") produces data of questionable value and badgers respondents unfairly.

That is not to suggest that hypothetical questions are always inappropriate. On the contrary, there are many situations in which hypothetical information would be useful, for example: "If this product came in smaller packages, would you consider buying it?" and "If you could be assured that this brand of frozen pizza *did* microwave better than others, would you consider paying extra for it?"

The trick is to recognize when respondents are being asked to make reasonable leaps of faith or contingency and when, by contrast, they are so constrained by circumstance or product orientation that no hypothetical assessment is truly meaningful.

DO NOT INTIMIDATE

Questions can be intimidating and counterproductive when they expose a participant's vulnerabilities or insecurities. If, for example, a question is asked that group members feel they should be able to answer but cannot, they may be provoked into hostility or silence. This is especially true when the question seems to address an area of the participant's expertise. Some physicians may feel professionally threatened when questions are posed about pharmaceutical products under their generic names rather than the better known brand names. Respondents who are asked if they have ever heard of a new concept or product may be challenged by the question to dissemble or withdraw.

It sometimes requires exquisite verbal adroitness to pose such questions without intimidating or embarrassing participants. In one group of pharmacists, a respondent mentioned that a particular fungicidal drug had a very broad spectrum of activity. Since this issue was of major interest in the study, the moderator asked the rest of the group "Did you all know that?" This question was particularly unfortunate because most of the pharmacists did *not* know it but felt that they should have, since the product in question was widely marketed.

The group interview, however, is not the method of choice for determining the extent of people's knowledge. While many group participants are secure enough to admit not knowing something that they "should," anonymous telephone or mail interviews are more appropriate data collection instruments when a key objective is establishing how widely something is known. If, however, it does become important to establish who in a group has a particular level of product knowledge, care must be taken to avoid offending or intimidating participants. Respondents must be given subtle permission to acknowledge their ignorance. In the previous illustration, the moderator might have said the following instead: "I have noticed in other groups that very few respondents seemed aware of this product's fungicidal spectrum. I wonder, how common is that knowledge?" Framing the question in this way would have allowed respondents to identify comfortably with the uninformed majority while in no way obliging them to claim ignorance.

BE ATTENTIVE TO PARTICIPANTS' BODY LANGUAGE

The ability to communicate attitudes with facial expressions, physical gesture and body position is widely recognized socially and well documented in the research literature[1,2,3] Group members may convey relevant information about their feelings and attitudes toward the topics being discussed, often without being aware of it themselves. The moderator must be constantly attentive to these gestural cues and be prepared to probe for their meaning if they appear to be relevant.

The participants who fold their arm across their chests and sit back in their chairs may be signaling withdrawal from the concept under discussion, and perhaps from the entire process. Those who roll their eyes heavenward in response to a concept without making comment are implying skepticism or cynicism that should not go unnoted. The group members who squint and furrow their brows may be communicating poor comprehension of the concept or some other confusion.

[1] R.L., Birdwhistell, *Kinesics and Context. Essays on Body Motion Communication* (Philadelphia, PA: University of Pennsylvania Press, 1970).

[2] E. Goffman, *Relations in Public* (New York, NY: Basic Books, Inc., 1971).

[3] J. Fast, *Body Language* (New York, NY: M. Evans 1970).

In a study of the acceptability of a new flooring material, a relatively silent group member was called upon by the moderator to comment upon one prototype design. Her comments were guardedly positive but clearly lacked any enthusiasm. Her facial expression conveyed that something concerned her. The moderator took note and reflected on her expression aloud, "You seem troubled by something." She responded by expressing reservations about the durability of the product, but could not be more explicit about what prompted the concern. While she spoke, she rubbed her thumb in a circular motion across her forefinger. The moderator commented on the gesture.

MODERATOR: I noticed that you were rubbing your fingers together like this (demonstrating) while you were talking. Did that have something to do with what you were saying?
PARTICIPANT: I guess so. I wonder if it would be crumbly after awhile. (Pause) It looks solid enough.
MODERATOR: Crumbly?
PARTICIPANT: Yeah, sort of, the design looks that way.

In this case the physical gesture conveyed a very relevant concern which the participant was reluctant to express verbally because it conflicted with the apparent physical properties of the material. Physical gestures are often employed to convey feelings that are difficult to articulate in words or to qualify, perhaps even contradict, an overt verbal response in some way.

The moderator has two responsibilities in decoding nonverbal cues. The first is to explore and clarify the meaning of their signals; the second is to record them in some fashion so that they become available to individuals who analyze the data. Though important, these obligations are not always easily met. While some nonverbal signals are widely recognized and understood, many researchers agree that the grammar and vocabulary of gestural communication are not always shared or correctly interpreted by all members of a culture. The moderator must also take care not to alienate or embarrass a respondent by calling attention to gestures in a way that implies that the respondent is entirely exposed or poorly controlled. Many gestures are subconsciously triggered and virtually invisible to those who make them. Participants who are hugging their chests or leaning back in their chairs are likely to feel uncomfortable or worse when a gesture of that sort is called to their attention.

On the other hand, the common parlance of body language—obvious facial expressions like frowns, rolled eyes, and so on—are generally safe and productive avenues of inquiry, for example, "I noticed you were frowning a moment ago . . . Why was that?" Attempts to probe gesture or facial expression not only uncover latent meanings but also encourage more conscientious participant introspection and convey the moderator's interest in externalizing every thought or feeling that is relevant to the discussion. Participants are likely to be flattered rather than made uncomfortable by attention to such expressions and overt gestures as long as the moderator conveys genuine interest in the participants' views and avoids the appearance of trapping them into revealing something they do not wish to expose.

PROBE FOR FEELING

Group participants do not know initially what level of motivational exploration is expected of them. Therefore, when asked to reflect on what led them to select the brands and products they do, many will provide superficial, socially acceptable responses. One way to pierce superficiality and to signal the moderator's interest in a more profound level of inquiry is to focus on feelings rather than rational thought in framing the questions.

In a study of gift giving, one group member described giving gifts to her parents as obligatory: "It's expected; they would be hurt if I didn't." Detailed description of her shopping behavior, however, made it clear that a lot of thought and caring went into her selection of gifts. The moderator wanted a better understanding of what prompted her selection of gifts and asked the participant to recount her *feelings*—when she shopped for the gifts, when she wrapped them and when she presented them. This request was met with more superficiality: "I felt good about it." The moderator then asked, "Do you ever tell your mother or father that you love them?" This question served as a key to unlock the obvious constraint in talking about her feelings toward her parents and the role that gifts play in expressing them. She acknowledged that she was emotionally very reserved and had great difficulty expressing strong feeling, especially to her parents. In her childhood, the expression of strong emotion was discouraged by her parents, to whom it represented lack of strength and control. Gifts symbolized the genuine love the participant felt for both her parents but conveyed the feeling in a controlled and protected way. The symbolism of the gift was masked even from the giver. It served both gift giver and recipient as a symbol of the affection neither could express openly without discomfort. These kinds of insights have proven useful time and again in developing advertising themes and executions centered around greeting card exchange and holiday giving.

USE DEPRIVATION QUESTIONS TO SHARPEN
PREFERENCES AND PRIORITIES

There are times when a direct question, even one that is succinctly and sharply phrased, simply does not yield a response in which the moderator has confidence. Under those circumstances the moderator should make use of questioning techniques which help to sharpen responses and provoke more vivid reactions. Deprivation, for example, is a technique that obliges respondents to make fine discriminations among a series of desirable options. One can ask a direct question such as "What are your favorite brands of beer?" but a question like that may encourage the participants to list all the brands they would accept, or perhaps all those that would be desirable under a variety of circumstances. If the research objectives require identifying the beer brand that is valued most of all, it may be more effective to pose a deprivation scenario, for example: "If you were vacationing in a cabin and could stock only one brand of beer, which one would you request?"

Imposing a realistic (though imagined) constraint on available options encourages more conscientious evalution of brands. It does not, however, necessarily reflect an entirely accurate or complete view of the market, in the sense that different brands or products may be favored for different ocasions. Thus, one should always remain sensitive to the risk of requiring that respondents name one favorite product. For a more thorough and valid understanding of market dynamics, respondents should be allowed to express a variety of situation-specific needs where relevant.

EXPLORE SPECIFIC USAGE OCCASIONS

A related technique for helping respondents recognize and articulate their purchase motivations is to question them in detail about the last time they bought a gift or ate a snack, or engaged in other activities pertinent to the subject. After a careful dissection of one such event or a succession of them, respondents may become more sensitive to their own needs and behaviors and better able to generalize in a meaningful way about what they do under many different circumstances. In the following illustration, the respondent was having difficulty generalizing about his food preferences and was therefore asked to build inductively on several recent snack occasions:

MODERATOR: Do you have any sort of general snack preferences—things you usually prefer at certain times?
RESPONDENT: Not really. It depends on the situation.
MODERATOR: On what specifically does it depend?
RESPONDENT: Oh, I don't know, my mood. What's available. What I've had recently.
MODERATOR: Okay, well let's talk about the last time you had a snack. When was that?
RESPONDENT: This afternoon . . . at about 3.
MODERATOR: What did you eat?
RESPONDENT: A bag of pretzels.
MODERATOR: What were you doing at the time?

RESPONDENT: I was doing my homework and got up to answer the phone so I took a break.

After pursuing the respondent's feelings at that time and the various other snack options considered, the moderator moved onto the preceding snack occasion. After a similar exchange, the respondent had a striking realization about his own behavior.

RESPONDENT: You know, now that I think of it—this is really strange—I think I tend to eat sweet snacks in the morning and salty snacks in the afternoon.
MODERATOR: What about in the evening?
RESPONDENT: Well, again, that depends.

In this next illustration drawn from a group of physicians, the respondent (a pontificator) insisted that his selection of drugs to treat asthma and other respiratory ailments (bronchodilators) depended entirely on patient characteristics and defied easy generalization. Through persistent probing, however, the moderator uncovered a sharp discrepancy between theory and practice.

MODERATOR: Let me describe a patient. I'm trying to select a type of patient that might be more common in the practice of a family practitioner. Someone that isn't very sick. Someone who has, say seasonal asthma; it lasts for several months with a few acute flare-ups during the rest of the year, and then they are pretty much Okay. Do you have patients like that?
DOCTOR: Sure, it sounds more like you're talking about allergy than asthma.
DOCTOR: Do you know you're jumping at spots which I don't think makes sense tonight, if I may interject. We've gone through the pharmacopeia of the treatment for asthma from A to Z. You haven't been specific as far as what to treat and how. An acute asthmatic? What age? And how about a complete examination?
MODERATOR: Assuming . . . ?
DOCTOR: You don't assume anything. You have to be a little bit more specific, if I may say so. We all, I think, are pretty much attuned on how to treat asthma patients. Are you going to see him in the emergency room for treatment in the hospital? That is entirely different than in the office except possibly injection of epinephrine which you would do in both places. Is the patient a patient of yours for 20 years or one month? Treatment is entirely different.
MODERATOR: The treatment is different?
DOCTOR: You know something about the patient. If the patient of yours is of one month, you might not have gone through a complete workup on the patient, you might not know what the cardio-

gram shows, or chest X-rays. Are we chest X-raying every one of these patients? What other medication are they taking? I think all these are most important when you're going to treat somebody who comes in with "asthma."

MODERATOR: Tell us about the last patient that you treated with a bronchodilator.

DOCTOR: The last one? I see at least two or three a day that I'll prescribe a bronchodilator. And every one might get a different one.

MODERATOR: How about the last one you saw?

DOCTOR: The last one I saw tonight? She came in with asthmatic bronchitis, coughing and spitting, had a cold about two weeks ago. We had her on some antibiotics at that time and when I saw her tonight in the office she had some wheezes and stuff like that. And I put her on a theophylline product and an antibiotic.

MODERATOR: How old is the patient?

DOCTOR: The patient is in her 40s.

MODERATOR: What if the patient were 25?

DOCTOR: If the patient were 25? With a history of what?

MODERATOR: Same patient—just younger.

DOCTOR: Younger? I would use the same thing. A theophylline product and also antibiotics. And make sure that they don't smoke.

MODERATOR: What if the patient were 60?

DOCTOR: 60? Antibiotics, for sure and I'd use theophylline but in a smaller dose. See how they get along. Have them call me back in two days and let me know how they're breathing and how they're coughing.

MODERATOR: Is this last patient you saw someone you had known for a long time?

DOCTOR: Oh sure, I know her about 20 years, maybe.

MODERATOR: And if you had just met her in your office, would you have prescribed something different?

DOCTOR: If I first met her in the office, if on examination, if I chest X-rayed and she didn't show anything in her lungs, if she hadn't run any temperature, and she wasn't what I had considered to be sick or septic, I might have just put her on some theophylline at that time.

MODERATOR: Basically it sounds like you use theophylline independent of how long you know the patient and independent of age.

DOCTOR: Well you see, when you use medication on somebody, I always tell them to call me in a couple of days, to let me know how the medication works. It's theophylline anyway you look at it.

MODERATOR: I was just curious. Didn't you say that age and familiarity with the patient matters a great deal in what medication you prescribe?

DOCTOR: Yes.

MODERATOR: It seems that no matter what the patient is like, if they wheeze they're going to get theophylline.

DOCTOR: Yes. True But it depends upon how much they wheeze.

Note that this respondent continued to insist that his treatment approach varied according to patient characteristics even when (gently) confronted with concrete evidence to the contrary. It was not, however, necessary or appropriate to convince the respondent of the inconsistency of his statements. Such self-revelations are not easy to induce, given the stability of people's self-images and their capacity for denial. Nor is it generally productive to demand that people confront the error of their deeply held views. In this case, the moderator's goal was served merely by exposing the discrepancy between belief and actual behavior. We want participants to remain psychologically intact, even if it sometimes means leaving them in a state of self-ignorance or self-deception.

One caution that should be raised about this technique is that it generally requires the moderator to question individual respondents intensively for sustained periods and in that respect, it tends to interrupt the interactive pattern of group exchange, at least temporarily. It requires skill and perseverance to reintegrate the group later when the moderator wishes interaction to resume, and there is always some risk that the group will resist. One way to forestall the problem is to alternate individual interrogations and full group discussions so that everyone is primed to expect a periodic resumption of group interaction.

INVENT HYPOTHETICAL SCENARIOS TO HELP
PARTICIPANTS CONCRETIZE RESPONSES

When respondents are reluctant to be specific or concrete, or perhaps they cannot because of limited product experience, the moderator may choose to abandon direct, personal questions in favor of hypothetical scenarios which allow respondents to express their feelings in less general and more evocative terms. Hypothetical scenarios can liberate both respondent and moderator from bland and uninformative generalities.

If, for example, the use of wine is the focus of discussion, the moderator may propose different scenarios in which wine may be served: a picnic, a small dinner party for eight intimate friends celebrating an anniversary, dinner with the boss, lunch at a neighborhood restaurant, a romantic dinner for two at home, and so on. The scenarios should be well developed and include all the elements that might conceivably influence the use of wine and choice of type, country of origin, price and brand.

Hypothetical scenarios are even more effective in group interviews with professionals because they provide a concrete point of departure for the ensuing discussion. With physicians, for example, what and how they prescribe often reflect a number of patient factors which must be made explicit if we are to understand their behavior.

VALIDATE CONCLUSIONS AND INTERPRETATIONS

The more effectively the moderator probes, the more comfortable he or she becomes with interpretations of what group members have been saying, and the more convinced he or she is about the conclusions that may be derived from the discussion. Despite that conviction, it is prudent to present them to the group for validation by saying, "This is what I think was said. If I have misinterpreted your comments or come to the wrong conclusion, tell me now." If there is a significant amount of disagreement with the moderator's conclusion, it is far better to expose it in the group than come away with serious misapprehensions.

Occasionally, deliberate misstatement or exaggeration can be used to sharpen or clarify responses or test the intensity of convictions. In one case, for example, the moderator summed up the group's opinions by saying, "Well I guess then, it's fair to say in conclusion that no ads to patients about prescription drugs are acceptable to you as physicians." Several respondents had already implied gingerly that *some* ads might be tolerated, but only when they heard their negative views stated (or overstated) in so unequivocal a fashion did they attempt to correct the moderator's misapprehensions and offer a more balanced perspective. It is often the most intransigent of respondents who rethink their position when extreme views are held up to them this way.

Probing Aids and Devices

Chapter 13

While most of the important issues in a group discussion can be thoroughly explored using verbal probes, there are situations in which a moderator may wish to call on other specialized questioning devices to elicit information that might not otherwise be fully articulated. It would perhaps be unfair to call these probing techniques nonverbal, since at very least they rely on some verbal instruction. They are, however, distinguished as a class from verbal probes by their reliance on psychological projection and metaphor to help participants recognize and communicate feelings or relationships that defy the average person's ability at description. Here are some examples:

SORTING TECHNIQUES

In order to understand what specifically prompts choice of a particular product, it is generally necessary to pursue the decision maker's understanding of the category as a whole: what products are placed in what category and how they are related to each other. Experience suggests that consumers may have a very different view of a market than those who provide a product or service. If identified, these differences can provide manufacturers with a clearer impression of the products against which they compete, thus offering important clues to more effective positioning.

Automobile manufacturers, for example, may view the market for passenger cars in relation to size, curb weight, price, model, and so on. Consumers, however, may classify cars on the basis of functions or styles ("dressy" vs. "sporty") and those categories sometimes confound best-laid marketing strategies. Thus, for example, the introduction of a sportier model of a classic four-door sedan many provoke dissonance or confusion by mixing signals and violating consumer car categories.

It is certainly possible to explore these perceptions by asking directly how respondents classify products and how they prioritize product features or dimensions when they consider the available options. A less direct, but sometimes more effective, way to address questions like these is via sorting procedures, in which we ask respondents to group common objects (products or brands) in whichever way they think appropriate.[1]

In a product sorting exercise, names of brands or specific models are printed on small cards and the respondent is given the following general instructions:

> Each of you has been given a deck of cards. Each card has the name of an automobile (Scotch, beer, antihypertensive, etc.) on it. Group the cards into piles, as many as you wish, so that those in any one group belong together— that is, have something in common with the others in that same group. You can make as many or as few groups as you like, and group the names in any way that makes sense to you. If you don't recognize a name, just put it into a separate group of names you don't know.

Group members who seek further guidance about what sorting categories can be used are reassured that they may sort in accordance with any principle they care to, and that there is no right or wrong way to do it.

Once sorting is completed, participants are asked what there is about each group of brands or models that suggested that they belong together. This procedure helps to illuminate which characteristics are most salient in a consumer's conceptual organization of the available products, while also identifying the competitive array for any brand.

For example, marketers of luxury cars would want to know whether the compact version of a Cadillac or Lincoln is grouped with other luxury models or with other compacts independent of price. Follow-up probing can determine whether the principles used to sort these cars have any impact on selection of a new car. Car owners who consign smaller luxury cars to the class of compacts might effectively exclude them from consid-

---

[1] Inspired by the Object Sorting Test of Kurt Goldstein & Martin Scheerer, which was designed to expose how different people develop concepts. Some people for example, group items on the basis of concrete sensory characteristics such as size, shape or color, while others sort by function or other more abstract dimensions.

eration because they are too cramped to qualify for "luxury" status or because their size compromises the status sought in a luxury car.

When this same sorting technique was applied to Scotch brands, participants were provided with miniature bottles of Scotch so that sorting could reflect cues other than name alone (such as label, bottle shape, and so on). The product groups that emerged and the probing that followed made clear what role is played by prestige, price, taste (heavy, light, smoky), and such factors as familiarity and inertia ("These are the ones I know," and "My family has served these two brands for years"). The same approach can be taken with any product label; some consumers may not recognize a marginal brand name but will immediately recognize the label.

The value of the sorting task is its ability to reveal perceptions of a category that are not necessarily available from direct inquiry, and may in fact be directly contradicted by what respondents themselves believe. In a group interview with physicians on tranquilizers, a physician stated unequivocally at the beginning of a group that a drug's duration of action—how long it works—was the single most important criterion of selection. He also said that he tended to use a wide variety of tranquilizers in order to match the duration of action with the needs of the patient.

When asked to sort tranquilizers into common groups, however, the physician sorted several and then stopped, appearing perplexed.

MODERATOR: Doctor, is something troubling you?
DOCTOR: I started off with the idea that I was going to sort by half-life and therefore long-lasting effects. As I got into it, I realized to my embarrassment that I wasn't really quite sure where some of these fit in. I sort of knew the ones I think of as being shorter, the ones I think of as being longer, and the ones I don't use so I don't know so much about them, I guess.
MODERATOR: You put only one in that group (pointing) and two in that group.
DOCTOR: That one is the only longer acting benzodiazepine I use and those two are both shorter acting ones. The others I don't know about at all. I guess that's why I don't use them.

The physician's initial comments would have led to the incorrect conclusion that he knew more about the duration of action of the drugs in this category and that his choice was a more deliberate and comprehensive one.

Note, however, that any assumptions or conclusions drawn on the basis of the groupings *should be validated, to the extent possible, by careful and extensive probing.* For example, even if physicians do not appear to use "potential for abuse" as a sorting criterion for tranquilizers, probing may reveal that this conspicuous omission reflects not disinterest but lack of differentiation: Physicians may simply view *all* tranquilizers as habituating to one degree or another. Thus, the sorting technique is merely a proce-

dure by which conceptual relationships among brands are externalized for
further examination by the moderator.

At the same time, the moderator or analyst must also recognize that
not only every finding can be verbalized or explicated by respondents, even
after sorting procedures have externalized their view of the market. There
will be instances in which the moderator must infer a rationale, as in the
example of a participant who has been asked to sort fruit preserves but
cannot put into words why he has classified peach flavor with orange but
grouped grape with apples (the rationale, as it happens, was a combination
of growing region and color). Indeed, it is in those very situations, when
relationships and perceptions are not easily verbalized, that sorting exercises prove most useful, either as a response stimulus, or as a response
substitute.

Information about how consumers group products may be especially
useful when markets are in a period of flux and "popular-priced" products
are attempting to gain premium status or new brands are vying for attention. Where, for example, did beer drinkers place Lowenbrau when it was
first produced in the U.S.? Was it placed with the premium imports or with
the domestic brands and if so, was it sorted with other Miller brands? The
participant who classified Lowenbrau with the Miller brands suggested, in
doing so, that he was acquainted with the marketer's brands and that the
family relationship was a salient component of its identity. Probing was
needed, however, to determine whether the corporate relationship enhanced or diminished its credibility.

Sorting techniques can also assist questionnaire development by fa-
miliarizing us with the language consumers use to designate product categories. For example, a segmentation study of the market for women's
casual clothes required an understanding of consumer clothing "taxon-
omy" so that appropriate terms could be employed in the questionnaire.
Relevant articles of clothing (blouses, jeans, dresses, and so on) were
sorted according to their primary function and the specific occasions on
which they would be most likely to be worn. When the sorting was complete, participants were asked to describe and name each group. If there
were differences among the participants in the way garments were sorted
or the category designations given, these differences became the focus of
subsequent discussion. By revealing and clarifying consumer terminology,
the discussions contributed significantly to the questionnaire-drafting
effort.

Where possible, there should be no fewer than 12 products or brands
to sort, and at least some of them should be similar to one another so that
there is a basis for common groupings. If respondents overlook those
similarities and place each brand or product in a group of its own, we have
clear evidence of market fragmentation.

Other variations on sorting techniques can be adapted for qualitative application to learn not only how consumers classify brands but also how far product lines may be extended without diluting brand strength. In one case, we provided respondents with names of eight food manufacturers and a long and varied list of food products ranging from breads and preserves to frozen dinners. Many of the manufacturers were specialty companies which presently market only two or three items on the list. We asked respondents to indicate which new products they would choose to buy from each manufacturer, exploring in detail why some brands could be extended further than others and why, for example, a maker of fruit preserves might successfully sell vegetables but not bread. That exercise revealed a great deal about the bounds of the brand's present equity as well as the relationship betwen neighboring product categories. Once again, however, it must be emphasized that the true value of these techniques often lies in the questioning opportunities they uncover. Without follow-up probing, the meaning of product classes and associations is not always fully understood.

PERSONIFICATION AND OTHER ANTHROPOMORPHIC PROJECTIVE TECHNIQUES

These techniques, which are actually another form of projection, seek to establish the image and character of a company or a brand by relating it to some well-known person, theatrical character or even animal. The approach helps participants communicate subtle characteristics of company or brand image that would otherwise require unusual verbal facility or insight. Occasionally, participants discover attitudes that are reflected in their personifications that surprise even themselves.

Personification reveals considerably more than merely positive or negative emotional valence. An automobile model personified by Michael Jackson conveys very different imagery than one that brings to mind James Bond or Archie Bunker. Of course, interpretation of the association requires that the moderator also probe the participant's image of the person to which brand is related. Michael Jackson may convey youth and vitality to some, sexual excitement to others, and glitzy excess to others. In all cases, however, it is important that the moderator set aside whatever predispositions he or she may have toward the personalities suggested and first attempt to uncover the participant's subconscious associations. In that sense, the use of personification (or anthropomorphication) is not necessarily a substitute for verbal description. Rather, it is a technique that helps participants recognize relationships they were unable to abstract and provides the moderator with a tighter focus for probing questions.

Subtle distinctions in imagery are possible with personification when it is accompanied by sensitive probing and subtle insight. To return to the automotive illustration, a sports car model that is related to Paul Newman by one group participant and to Steve McQueen by another is determined by probing to reflect the speed and excitement associated with auto racing (Newman) and cinema car chases (McQueen). The difference is that something menacing, a sort of controlled hostility, is conveyed by the McQueen characterization that is absent in the Newman association. A participant may be unable to articulate those differences when describing the models but may provide a wealth of imagery when relaying feelings about the actors who personify them. Of course, to a car manufacturer, distinctions of this kind have important advertising implications, one facet or the other can be reinforced or softened to achieve the desired market positioning.

In one study undertaken to assess several alternative campaigns for a financial corporation, one option focused upon the headquarters building itself, a very tall, narrow structure with striking and unusual architecture.* The copy spoke of the strength, breadth and power of the company. Some women reacted very negatively to this campaign concept, however, offering personified associations like "Attilla the Hun" and "Genghis Khan" to suggest a rapacious and threatening (phallic?) quality that was totally incongruous with the protective, supportive image the company intended to project.

Animals to which we attribute human motivation may serve equally well as a projective device to yield clues about perceived image of products and companies. To explore the image of an equipment manufacturer and its competitors, respondents were asked to suggest animals that could stand for or represent each company in turn. (Another way of asking the question might be: "Imagine that in a dream, perhaps, the Acme Company was turned into an animal—any animal, real or legendary. What animal would the Acme Company be?")

This technique permits a more incisive understanding of image distinctions among companies that seem superficially quite similar. The two dominant companies in this market were each viewed as large, powerful, successful and effective in servicing their market. Verbal descriptions gave little basis for distinguishing them.

When requested to characterize the two companies in terms of animals, however, one was more frequently associated with lions and the other with tigers. The interpretation of these associations rests on what these animals represent to the respondents who offered them. We made no automatic assumptions about the consensual meaning of these symbols, but in probing the projections further, it became clear that the lion symbolized regal dignity, confidence and leadership while the tiger suggested equal power and dominance, but exercised in a more aggressive and predatory manner.

*Cited with permission of Transamerica Corporation

Associations to other competitors were equally revealing. One company was associated with a teddy bear, an image that suggested the ingratiating friendliness of the company's sales representatives but reflected little respect. Other companies were seen as a mole (". . . because the salesman always goes around me to the boss"), a bat ("They do all their business by mail; like bats they hide in dark caves"), a snake (". . . can't trust them"), and a unicorn ("People know about them, but you never see them").

There is no rule of thumb to guide the selection of animals or people and personalities for projection. The moderator must rely on instinct and personal experience in making that selection. However, if the technique is well applied, either approach can be extremely productive. Respondents using such techniques seem to suspend the censor that operates more rigorously when asked to verbalize perceptions, especially those which they believe are small, insignificant, irrational or unsubstantiated.

STEREOTYPED DRAWINGS AND PHOTOGRAPHS

These devices have consistently been among the most useful of all of the projective techniques designed to probe subconscious attitudes. The stimuli can be either artist's sketches or stock head and shoulder portraits. We prefer sketches because of the far greater freedom they permit in customizing the stereotypes to the needs of the study.

In one study designed to explore the image of a domestic beer brand, the client had expressed concern that his brand had become associated with rural, politically conservative, and racially intolerant older men. To explore the various facets of this brand image, stereotypic pictures as shown in Figures 1, 2, and 3, were drawn to depict particular components.

These custom-drawn stereotypes were included in the standard sterotype portfolio that had been used for many years. Participants were asked to select the beer drinkers depicted in the stereotypes who would be most likely to prefer the client's brand. Participants were also asked to select people who would prefer what was perceived to be the principal competitor.

Stereotype selection, in this case, was so consistent that it confirmed the existence of an image problem and further defined its nature. This exploratory procedure was also invaluable in providing guidance for the survey that followed. Not only did it identify the most relevant image dimensions to quantify, it also directed us to the selection of specific stereotypes for use in the questionnaire.

Another study about snack products was approached with the assumption that because snack behavior is routine (yet so complex), consumers might have difficulty recognizing and articulating their own moti-

NATIONAL ANALYSTS-
A DIVISION OF
BOOZ·ALLEN ʅ HAMILTON INC.

FIGURE 1.

vations. This was indeed the case, but through the use of projective pictures, it became apparent that many snack products have deep-rooted social and demographic associations which respondents had difficulty expressing without the appropriate stimulus material.

It was learned, for example, that some snacks are associated with sophisticates, some with teens, some with small children, and so on, and that these images shape not only general product acceptability but also the circumstances under which various snacks are seen as appropriate. Those

NATIONAL ANALYSTS-
A DIVISION OF
BOOZ·ALLEN ₤ HAMILTON INC.

FIGURE 2.

responsible for testing a series of new snack ideas were better able to position them based on this information.

Stereotypes can also be used as a customized thematic apperception test (T.A.T.). Participants might be asked how the women pictured in Figures 4 and 5 feel about baking from scratch (or purchasing generic rather than branded products, drinking superpremium light beer brands, and so on). The participant is encouraged to elaborate fully on how the

National Analysts –
A Division Of
Booz·Allen ¢ Hamilton Inc.

FIGURE 3.

stereotyped women regard the products and the brands, in what situations they would be used, when they would be avoided and why they would select or reject certain brands.

Like any projective technique, this one liberates participants from inhibitions about expressing their own preferences or opinions, while also concretizing associations they might not be able to express without the aid of pictures.

FIGURE 4.

FIGURE 5.

SERIAL FREE ASSOCIATION

In this technique, participants are requested to say whatever comes to mind in association with a brand, product concept, or company. Use of the technique assumes that the chain of uncensored associations will lead to insights not attainable by more direct inquiry.

A study that sought to understand the enduring appeal of the Budweiser team of Clydesdale horses may serve as an example in which useful insights were revealed by means of serial free association.* When the topic was first introduced, a group of blue-collar workers readily expressed their great appreciation of the Clydesdales. Asked what there was about these massive horses that pleased them, participants talked principally about how handsome they were and how they provoked imagery of a romantic and traditional past. These rather pallid responses hardly seemed sufficient to account for their enthusiasm, much less to sustain the popularity of the Clydesdale symbol over many years. Was there more underlying the appeal of these symbols than what was immediately accessible to conscious exploration?

Serial association led the group along a preconscious trail of ideas and images that revealed an interesting hypothesis. For this blue-collar group, Clydesdales symbolized many of the virtues they most valued in themselves. First, the Clydesdales are workers; each of them pulls a fair share of the load. They work in a team with others like themselves rather than competing or laboring individually. They are brawny, powerful and tough, not effete, fragile, spindly-legged race horses. Despite their role as workers, however, they are clearly aristocratic in their bearing and grooming. To these blue-collar workers, the Clydesdales represented a unique symbol of the worker-aristocrat, honored for superior strength and dignity.

While provocative and important insights like these make serial free association a useful technique in the moderator's arsenal, it suffers handicaps which remand it to infrequent, specialized use. First, few participants seem able to free associate. Free association is a skill that has to be learned, and the customary two-hour group is not always an appropriate or adequate environment for instruction. Participants may offer one or two fairly predictable, shallow associations and go no further. It is a rare participant with the confidence, diligence and intelligence to sustain successful free association. Even those few group members who *can* comply may be reluctant to risk exposing potentially revealing, embarrassing or ego-dystonic thoughts in a public setting.

Finally, the insights that emerge from this procedure are often so idiosyncratic that they yield few actionable implications. Thus, while intellectually challenging, the effort required is not usually justified by the outcome.

*Quoted with permission of Anheuser-Bush, Inc.

MUSIC

The enormous differences between the commanding opening theme of Strauss' "Thus Spake Zarathustra," or "Ode to Joy" in Beethoven's glorious *Ninth Symphony* and the delicate confectionery of Mozart's "Eine Kleine Nachtmusik" present an opportunity to capture the feeling implicit in product imagery or advertising themes. This technique is especially helpful in studies that seek to expose latent attitudes and feelings toward brands or companies that are subtle, difficult to express verbally, or likely to be only marginally conscious.

In a study of the differences in image among domestic premium beer brands, effort was devoted to accessing not only those ideas that are easily identified and easily expressed, but also those that reside just below full consciousness. With the aid of a musicologist, dozens of brief snatches of music were selected that seemed to convey emotions that could be associated with beer brands. These were pretested for their ability to provoke feelings relevant to beer (such as "dignified," "exciting," "dominant," "weak," "wimpy," "gutsy"). Musical stimuli that provoked only vague evaluative comments (such as "nice," "interesting") were discarded. This process resulted in an audio tape of twenty pieces of music, each several seconds in length.

These musical stimuli were used in the same way that stereotypic drawings or photographs are used. Group members were asked to relate musical excerpts to whatever beer brands came to mind, or conversely to select those excerpts that best represented the brand under investigation. Preliminary testing had already linked a series of verbal descriptions with each excerpt so that it was possible to move beyond musical imagery to more familiar denotative language.

Although the technique has been productive, one major handicap is the difficulty it poses for participants. While some can relate music to brands, many others cannot reach that level of abstraction and creativity. The moderator's request may provoke only nervous giggles, perplexed stares, or superficialities. It also requires an inferential translation from musical concepts to verbal ones—a translation which respondents should not be asked to make. When it works well, however, as it does with very creative and intelligent group participants, it can yield subtle and rewarding insights.

RATING SCALES

A key goal of qualitative research is to learn not only what motivations shape consumer behavior, but also how likely consumers are to accept new products and services or how strongly committed they are to existing ones.

In addressing those questions, moderators have at their disposal the arsenal of probing techniques described earlier but, in some cases, they may not be entirely convinced that they know whether consumers would actually purchase a product if it were to become available. Qualitative research permits a gratifying richness and flexibility of expression, but the penalty we pay is a linguistic imprecision that sometimes tempts us to borrow the techniques of quantitative measurement. Therefore, it is not unusual for a moderator to poll respondents, often at the end of the session, in order either to force them to communicate the intensity of the view (on a scale from 1 to 10). Customarily, participants respond on a piece of paper and then reveal their answers after the exercise has been completed in order to minimize intragroup contamination.

We generally reserve polls, if we use them, for a point near the end of the session so that the responses reflect whatever processes of evaluation and persuasion were ongoing in the session. While these quantitative devices can be useful, it is essential that their rationale and their limits be fully understood. When we press quantitative techniques into the service of group interviews, we are not aiming to tally participant reactions; we are merely using widely stated quantitative conventions to clarify what we heard respondents tell us verbally. Rating scores or votes of this kind can serve as a platform for further summary probing to help the moderator better grasp the relationship between expressions of interest and actual purchase projections. It is entirely inappropriate, however, to average or otherwise manipulate these numbers.

We also take strong exception to the practice of polling group participants serially on everything from purchase behavior to brand familiarity and then probing their responses in order to better understand them. Some researchers with an unwarranted fear of group contamination judge this type of hybrid session to be a well-managed group. Though certainly "managed," it more closely approximates our definition of a serial interview than a group. We submit that it offers few if any advantages, precisely because it limits the opportunity for group interaction and it rigidifies a process whose strength lies in spontaneity.

Neither of these approaches is to be confused with mini-surveys, sometimes taken before and after group sessions to capitalize on what may be a total sample of 40 to 60 individuals. These "surveys," which may or may not relate to the actual goal of the group sessions, are acceptable so long as they do not compromise the qualitative research by sensitizing participants to key issues in advance. A decision about whether to begin or end with a survey (if it is on a subject related to the group) must be made on a case-by-case basis, taking into account the topics addressed and the questions asked. In general, however, we believe greater pains should be taken to safeguard the group methodology than the informal add-on survey.

CONFRONTATIONAL TECHNIQUES

While rating scales can provide a springboard for evaluating intensity of feeling, it is sometimes necessary to resort to more pointed and decisive tests of product loyalty and conviction.

The concept of product loyalty is often invoked to explain consumer resistance to switching to other brands or categories of products. We submit, however, that loyalty is a behavioral and not a motivational concept. It describes what people do, not why they do it. Research is sometimes needed to explore these motivations more carefully in order to understand how truly vulnerable a product or brand may be.

Behavioral consistency (or product loyalty for those who prefer the traditional term) reflects one of two intervening motivational variables: product inertia and product commitment. The consumer driven by inertia or experience is merely seeking to avoid product decisions and therefore is likely to continue selecting the same ones based on reflex or inertia until something forcibly disrupts this repetitive pattern.

There are, however, consumers who select the same product over and over again because they are convinced that the product is in some way superior to others. The motivational foundation of their consistency in product selection is a conscious commitment to the attributes of the product itself. Clearly, these different levels of commitment have implications for the marketer who seeks either to sustain inertia or to undermine it. When degree of motivational commitment is of interest, the following techniques may be useful:

Devil's Advocacy

To test the extent to which a group participant clings to an expressed attitude or feels allegiance to a product, the moderator may abandon a stance of dispassionate remoteness and present arguments that challenge the participant's views. For example, the moderator may present the arguments of a salesman or remind the participant of product attributes that have been overlooked in order to provoke a reassessment of earlier opinions. This procedure is especially useful when the marketer wishes to devise promotional strategies to counter or preempt competitive arguments. While this technique is useful in establishing the relevance and persuasiveness of counter arguments and in testing the participant's commitment to a particular point of view, it poses some methodological risks.

The major risk is that the moderator may be seen as so firmly allied with the product in question that the role of objective researcher is seriously compromised. Participants may be less candid and perhaps less cooperative in sharing their thoughts and feelings with a moderator who is seen as an advocate of a particular point of view.

Actually some moderators so value devil's advocacy that they elevate it to a confrontational mode. They aggressively challenge the positions taken by group members, not only risking anger but deliberately provoking it.[2] They contend that more profound discussions are provoked by a charged group atmosphere than by a sedate and emotionally neutral one.

However successful they may sometimes be, we believe that extreme confrontational tactics are never justified, particularly in view of the other methodological options available. Group respondents are volunteers in a process convened for the benefit of researchers and their clients. It is our ethical responsibility, and it is also in our best interests, to avoid any deliberate abuse of that cooperation in the interests of research.

Moderator's Accomplice

If the moderator is convinced of the value of a confrontational approach in a particular set of groups, an accomplice can be enlisted who poses as a member of the group and assumes the role of "agent provocateur." The moderator's accomplice obviates the need for devil's advocacy since he or she becomes, in effect, the devil.

The moderator's accomplice may be employed to test both commitment to traditional consumer buying patterns and resistance to those that are socially unpopular or innovative. In one such study, we enlisted a pair of accomplices to help us explore consumers' rejection of ceramic tile flooring for certain nontraditional applications.

Ceramic tile has been well received in some functional areas of the home (such as the kitchen) and frequently rejected in others (living room, bedroom). A series of group depth interviews were conducted to explore the motivations that shaped these behaviors and the intensity of the resistance to ceramic tile in certain sections of the home.

A research procedure was sought that would not only expose how consumers feel about selecting flooring for their home, but would also permit closer examination of the process by which the selections are made. Ideally, we would have convened our research in the homes of those actively involved in decorating and listened in as homeowners discussed their needs and options. The next best alternative was to simulate a home decorating task in the group interview context.

A table-top two bedroom model home was constructed, and three sets of model furniture (colonial, traditional and contemporary styling) were designed and handmade for all rooms. All of the other requisite decorating accessories (paint, wallpaper, flooring, lamps, appliances, and so on) were also provided in a wide variety of colors, materials and patterns.

Four married couples were invited to each group and asked to deco-

[2]Myril D. Axelrod, "The Dynamics of the Group Interview," *Advances in Consumer Research*, 3, (1976) 437–441.

rate the home in accordance with their own design preferences. As each couple decorated the model home, other couples were invited to comment on the selection and ask questions about decorating decisions. One couple, however, were the moderator accomplices. One or the other accomplice would inquire into virtually every flooring choice made by the other participants, forcing them to reflect on what led to their flooring selection.

When the accomplices themselves were asked to decorate, they selected a patterned ceramic flooring for the living room and a quarry tile for the bedroom, both unconventional flooring choices. After completing the decorating, they excused themselves and left, attributing their early departure to a previous commitment which they had announced to the group at the outset. The other group members were thus free to be as critical as they wished of the accomplices' selections without risk of injuring feelings or giving offense.

In this way, the accomplices served to challenge the allegiance of group members to traditional flooring concepts and provoked a spontaneous discussion about the intensity of their resistance to untraditional alternatives. The care with which each decorating task was undertaken and the heated exchanges both between husband and wife and among the couples, confirmed that the technique produced a conscientious effort and an expression of genuine and intense feeling. The method provided unusual access to the decision-making process and the motives that shape them. It is costly, however, and should be reserved for studies that have far-reaching strategic implications when other more orthodox approaches are unlikely to be as illuminating.

The benefits of confrontation can be achieved with less contrivance by structuring groups so that they include both antagonists and protagonists of relevant brands and products. In a study of cake mixes, for example, some group members might be make-from-scratch bakers, while others might be recruited from among those who use packaged cake mixes. The goal of exposing the perceived assets and liabilities of prepared cake mixes is aided by the confrontation between those who accept them and those who do not. From this interchange insights emerge that contribute to the development of new product ideas and more effective product positioning. Clients who worry that heterogeneity of this sort may be intimidating overlook the very real benefit of testing convictions under challenge, and underestimate the ability of an experienced moderator to maintain a discussion that is lively and controversial but not threatening or destructive.

More elaborate techniques for bringing together widely divergent groups of consumers have been developed in France, where one research agency conducts two groups simultaneously in different rooms. Each of the groups is recruited to reflect opposing views or divergent market behavior. After each of the groups have had an opportunity to explore their own attitudes in separate sessions, they are brought together (by closed circuit TV) and invited to discuss their different views with one another. The confrontation provides an interesting test of the conviction with which attitudes are held.

Role Playing

In the course of doing a group, if the moderator wishes to test which arguments are most effective in switching a committed or inertia-driven consumer to another product, a participant may be asked to take the role of antagonist. The antagonist must be chosen with care for the technique to be effective. Ideally, the antagonist-participant should be outspoken, confident and represent a view that is genuinely divergent. It helps if the antagonist relishes a license to argue.

False Labeling

Some consumers adopt product or brand prejudices with such devotion that the task of modifying their commitment becomes monumental. Paradoxically, this may be especially true in cases where competing products or brands have very similar intrinsic characteristics and are distinguished only by intangible or ascribed image attributes. Under those circumstances, marketers may profit from careful exploration of brand intransigence.

As we have already noted, beer is one such product category. Some beer drinkers are convinced that their favorite brand of domestic, premium-priced beer is clearly distinguishable from and superior to all others. A competitor planning an advertising campaign that is designed to woo adherents of that brand may be justifiably concerned about whether this goal is a realistic one. Before embarking on that effort, a marketer should know the breadth and the intransigence of consumer brand commitment.

In one such study, in which brand commitment to market leaders was the central issue, participants were served two glasses of the *same* beer in sequence during the course of the session. The first glass of beer was identified as one of the dominant premium domestic brands. The second glass was identified as their personal favorite. With few exceptions, participants accepted the deception and proceeded to describe the differences in accordance with previously discussed attributes. This experience, repeated in several groups, conveyed the extent to which accumulated brand imagery apparently dominated sensory perception. Confronting participants with the deception after the fact is inadvisable, however, since it contributes little or nothing to the research and undermines the moderator-group rapport.

A similar case, having to do with garment fibers, illustrates the same basic point. Fabrics made of manmade fibers have traditionally had difficulty achieving the status and acceptability of natural fibers in some end-use categories. This has been especially true in men's business and dress garments. To better understand the attributes distinguishing manmade and natural fibers, men's slacks were alternatively identified as having contents of 100 percent wool or a blend containing some polyester. The fiber contents in all of the garments were, in fact, identical.

When asked which of the garments they preferred and what prompted this preference, participants accepted without question manmade blends of 100 percent natural fabrics and slacks made of wool as blends. In describing the basis for their selection, many relied on perceived sensory characteristics (texture, weight, and so on) of the fiber content to justify their evaluation.

These outcomes confirm the extent to which most people will selectively seek to reinforce rather than challenge or modify the views they always hold—a principle known as dissonance reduction. The true value of these deceptive techniques, however, lies in the fact that not all views are so zealously guarded. Respondents will sometimes acknowledge a similarity between two products previously thought to be quite different and will work to restructure their views in accordance with new information. Group interviews can be used to help distinguish the uphill battles from the easy skirmishes.

As a general rule, the techniques which are most widely and easily utilized are those which require the least preparation. Verbal probes, of course, remain the most accessible and spontaneous, but projective devices like personification and stereotype pictures also require little advance preparation. A stock set of projective pictures can be maintained and used for many different studies with little or no modification. (Of course, customized drawings should be commissioned when appropriate.) Projects thought to touch on especially subtle issues should be reviewed with one or several of the more specialized techniques in mind.

The value of utilizing both verbal and nonverbal probing techniques to explore image dimensions that reside in the less accessible regions of the preconscious or unconscious is especially well illustrated in a study of the Coors mystique conducted some years ago.* In the early 1970s, Coors beer enjoyed a unique cachet among domestic brands, particularly among beer drinkers who lived in states where Coors was unavailable or difficult to get. We encountered group interview participants who had gone to extraordinary lengths to acquire Coors for themselves or provide it for others. Some had made pilgrimages to neighboring states within the Coors trading area and returned with cases for distribution to friends and relatives. It had been rumored that even President Ford brought back cases of Coors on Air Force One on forays into Coors trading territory.

To explore the elements of this powerful image, a series of group depth interviews was conducted, both within the Coors trading areas and just outside its periphery. Two components of the Coors image emerged

*Quoted with permission of The Stroh Brewery Company

readily without recourse to projective stimuli. A principal component of the Coors image was its reputation as lighter in taste and less bloating than competitive beers. The high regard for Coors' alleged lightness was at the time consistent with a trend toward lightness in alcoholic beverages, reflected in the increasing popularity of white wines and white liquors (such as gin and vodka). In retrospect, it seems reasonable to suppose that this appreciation for Coors' lightness may have presaged the market's readiness to accept the introduction of light beers.

Another major component of Coors imagery was the high quality implied by its single brewery in Colorado and by its refrigeration from production to delivery. Though positive images to be sure, these elements of the Coors' reputation did not in themselves seem to warrant the extraordinary cachet enjoyed by Coors among its most dedicated followers. In fact, further exploration revealed that other beer brands were also associated with lightness and high quality.

Was the Coors mystique attributable to its perceived exclusivity, valued as a proprietary brand by those who could obtain it in their region and desired by those who could acquire it only as a sort of contraband brew? When probed, Coors regional exclusivity *did* emerge as a relevant factor, but group members noted that there were many other regional brands equally inaccessible outside of their trading area, and some even shared the same light character and high quality.

What, then, would account for the remarkable appeal of Coors during this period? In order to help group members communicate the sensory, affective, nonrational and nonverbal aspects of beer brand imagery, a variety of projective stimuli were employed. These included stereotyped pictures, musical excerpts and nonrepresentational lines in rounded, angular and wavy shapes.[3] These analyses suggested a brand personality in which the dominant components were:

> *Escape and relaxation,* the absence of pressure, tension or competition, a tranquil pristine environment, and
>
> *Individuality,* the prospect of finding one's own way and eschewing lockstep conformity.

Essential in establishing these personality characteristics was Coors' theme of pure Rocky Mountain spring water, usually visualized as a rushing mountain stream between snow covered banks amidst crisp, fresh air. These sensory associations were common in the fantasy provoked by the projective techniques.

In particular, it became apparent that the Coors' imagery addressed powerful needs of the uban, blue-collar beer drinker. The symbolism of

---

[3] For explanation of this rarely used technique, see: A.E. Goldman, "Symbolic Representation in Schizophrenia," *Journal of Personality,* 28, no. 3 (September 1960), 293–316

Rocky Mountain spring water promised escape from the crowding, anonymity, and pollution of urban life, and the stress and tension that often go
along with it. As one of the more articulate group members put it: "You're
actually buying a nonprescription tranquilizer; a legal high—fresh air,
pure water and a babbling brook in your can of Coors." These insights
were extremely useful in helping to understand the fundamental basis for
the brand's extraordinary success—something which is not always fully
understood by those who compete against a product, or even by those who
market it themselves.

Moderator Characteristics and Training Requirements

Chapter 14

PERSONAL STYLES

Previous chapters focus on the techniques employed by the moderator in conducting groups. This one addresses not what the moderator does but the style in which he or she does it. While fledgling moderators can be taught most of the techniques of group moderating, their individual styles are shaped by personality factors not readily altered by training.

Some basic guidelines for moderator behavior have already been suggested. The moderator must be pleasant, accepting, supportive, and above all, scientifically dispassionate regarding the issues explored in the group. He or she must also display obvious confidence and comfort with the role of questioner and group leader. An individual who betrays anxiety about the right to lead the group or to probe for information may forfeit authority in the early stages of the discussion and find participants unresponsive or even hostile. A good journalist and a good moderator both know that respondents take their cues from the interviewer. If the interviewer communicates discomfort in asking a question, respondents will suspect that they need not, or should not, answer it.

Within those broad guidelines, however, there is considerable room for individual variation. Moderating styles differ and it is entirely appropriate that they should. Trainees who violate their own personality in an attempt to mimic the style of a respected mentor may convey insincerity and discomfort, jeopardizing the formation of a true group. Moderators are encouraged to find a style with which they are personally comfortable, whether that be serious intensity, lighthearted joviality or something in between. There are, however, some styles of group moderating that may compromise the quality of the results and may actually exploit or abuse the participants. Several such moderator "types" are described here.

The Intimidating Moderator

Just as there are intimidating participants, there are also intimidating moderators. Intimidation may serve diverse personal motives, among which aggression is perhaps the most powerful. We do not mean to imply that anyone with aggressive needs cannot become an effective moderator. We do submit that aggressive impulses not otherwise sublimated or controlled are likely to be destructive. Some participants may be challenged to engage the moderator in a covert struggle to express power, while others may simply retire from the group in response to the moderator's intimidation.

The Authoritarian Moderator

If the moderator's need to control and manipulate others is so dominant that it suppresses participant spontaneity and interchange, then the research objectives of the study may be subverted. The need to control a group is not destructive in itself but it may become damaging when the expression of that need intrudes upon or extinguishes relevant participant interaction.

The Exhibitionist Moderator

The moderator who uses the group primarily as an opportunity to enhance his or her own ego by seeking to elicit admiration gives priority to personal needs before those of the research. One variation on this theme is the moderator who seeks approval of the group or observers by being excessively or exploitatively humorous. A witty remark or pun can be used constructively to reduce interpersonal tension in the group, deflect anger or merely brighten a somber or boring discussion. For example, when a physician noted that a leading antiulcer medication "filled a big hole," the moderator queried, "In the stomach or in the market?" and that seemed to relax a tense group and encourage more vigorous participation. Humor becomes intrusive, however, when its principal motive is to focus attention on the moderator's wit or skill as a humorist. Properly recruited participants expect to be interviewed, not entertained.

The use of humor can also become destructive if it causes participant discomfort. A group member interrupted the conversation several times to ask questions about who was sponsoring the research, how it was to be used, and who was behind the one-way mirror. Each time the moderator answered the question sincerely without violating client anonymity. When, however, the participant interrupted the discussion a fourth time to ask who would receive the audio tapes, an exasperated moderator said with a smile, "The CIA." The moderator's sarcasm drew laughter from the group—probably because they, too, had grown weary of the suspicious inquiries—but the chastened participant was offended and withdrew from further involvement.

The Seductive Moderator

A male moderator who leads a group of women or a female moderator leading a group of men must guard against subtle, unintentionally seductive behavior. Although male participants may receive it more good naturedly and less defensively than women, seductive behavior by either male or female moderators is at best distracting, and will almost certainly diminish or distort the results of the research.

The Voyeuristic Moderator

Intellectual curiosity is one of the driving motivations of any good moderator. To be effective, one has to take genuine pleasure in learning about the small details and nuances of people's behavior and attitudes. At the same time, a moderator whose group management is driven by prurient interest jeopardizes the research and violates the privacy of participants in order to gratify personal needs. Most group topics do not explore intimate or delicate subject matter, but the moderator must always excercise caution and restraint when dealing with those that do. The moderator is also advised to safeguard the group against the sexual voyeurism or exhibitionism of individual members. Although some members may choose to talk about their use of ordinary skin care products to promote or elicit sexual feelings, that same type of delicate disclosure should not be asked or required of others unless they volunteer it.

MODERATOR DEMOGRAPHICS

The selection of a moderator for a particular series of groups frequently reflects at least passing consideration of demographic characteristics. In the early days of group interviewing, those who hired or assigned moderators adhered to principles of selection that have largely been abandoned today. It was held that women should not lead groups of men in a discussion of traditionally male or macho topics (for instance, beer, men's clothing, trucks, industrial products) because it was felt that men would not be

candid with women about the distinctively male needs these products gratify, nor would they talk in the informal, sometimes off-color language that
some men use in the presence of other men.

Women were also discouraged from conducting discussions with
physician or senior executive groups on the assumption that women could
not command the needed authority to manage so forceful a group.
Another frequent argument for rejecting women moderators was their
presumed ignorance about industrial or technical products. In nearly
every case, these arguments reflected a sexist logic that made better myth
than methodology.

One study which illustrates that point involved a series of groups on
the factors governing selection of truck chassis and engines, all conducted
(as per research protocol) by a male moderator. Although the moderator
was both experienced and professionally able, four groups yielded superficial platitudes and very little real insight.

In exploring reasons for the disappointingly shallow outcome, the
moderator's supervisor detected a reluctance on the part of the moderator
to pursue issues that required assertive probing. Perceiving an obligation to
know about such macho things as cylinder displacement and axle ratios, the
moderator was evidently unwilling to expose his lack of sophistication
about the subject matter by asking pertinent questions. Even a careful
briefing on the topic had failed to allay his insecurity. Apparently the male
group members participated in this deceit by assuming that a man would,
or should, be conversant with truck specifications.

In the spirit of experimentation, a woman moderator was assigned
the same task and given the same preparation. From the outset, she acknowledged to the group her limited knowledge of truck products, and
solicited their help in explaining things that she might not understand. The
macho posturing or patronizing attitude that might have been expected in
the presence of a woman was never displayed. Patiently and incisively,
group members explored the reasons for their selection decisions, offering
insights absent from the first series of male-moderated groups.

The lessons to be learned from this experience are twofold. First,
moderators who fail to clarify relevant issues in order to mask ignorance
protect their egos at the expense of the research results. Second, assumptions about the appropriateness of inviting a woman moderator to conduct
groups on supposedly male subjects are frequently unjust. While it may be
true that men often feel compelled to "clean up" their language for a
female moderator, we are not convinced that something crucial is necessarily lost when they do that. Colloquial language does not necessarily guaran-
tee either candor or insight.

Similarly, there is no reason to assume that men cannot lead fruitful
discussions on subjects regarded as traditionally female. Men have successfully conducted groups on topics related to homemaking, grooming, and

childcare without difficulty even during an era when these subjects were unequivocally the province of women. Shifting sex roles have, of course, blurred these boundaries. However, it is still generally desirable to match the sex of moderator and participants in discussions on intimate topics that might otherwise cause embarrassment or discomfort. Even here, however, a capable and nonseductive moderator may elicit surprising admissions. For example, in one group session with male hypertension patients, a participant acknowledged experiencing impotence problems as a result of his medication in the presence of a female moderator.

A similar question often asked is whether young moderators are handicapped in leading groups of much older participants. Experience suggests that any difficulty that may be experienced is more dependent upon the social maturity and poise of the moderator than upon age per se. A very young moderator is, however, likely to be handicapped in conducting a group composed of participants whose professional attainments have accorded them some exalted status in society. Thus, a group of chief executive officers of large corporations or a group of nationally-known physicians may feel that a young moderator lacks the stature or experience appropriate to their own.

Age may, however, be a more serious handicap when an older moderator conducts a group session with teenagers. Teenage groups pose special difficulties because their extreme self-consciousness and rather narrow, sometimes intolerant definition of age peers can discourage group formation in a brief two hours. In their characteristic reticence, teen respondents may be rebelling against adult authority or proceeding on the assumption that anyone "old" cannot understand their needs and lifestyle. Sometimes younger moderators have greater success with teenagers but a teen group is difficult to conduct under any circumstances. The social discomfort and introversion so frequently exhibited by early teens in group interviews tend to argue for consideration of individual interviews instead.

Race and ethnicity are also given frequent (though not always appropriate) consideration in selecting a moderator. Indeed, for many years, one of the most widely accepted premises in group moderating was that groups of black participants are best led by a black moderator. The same is claimed today for Hispanic groups.

There may have once been a time when the cultural and psychological gulf between a white moderator and a group of ethnic participants was too difficult for most people to bridge. We believe, however, that today an experienced white or Anglo moderator can effectively conduct group sessions with blacks or Hispanics as long as he or she is sensitive to the moderating problems that may arise as a result of cultural distance. It has been argued that the striking heterogeneity of the Hispanic-American community makes matching moderator to participants suprisingly delicate and difficult. A moderator who speaks Puerto Rican Spanish may be more disadvantaged than a Hispanically "neutral" Anglo when facing a group of Chicanos or Cuban-Americans.

Experience has also shown that conspicuously upscale blacks whose speech, personal style, and profession communicate that they have "made it" can be more intimidating than a white moderator to a group of ordinary black consumers. The white moderator is expected to be an outsider, less culturally "sympatico" and less familiar with the relevant slang than someone who shares the same ethnic origins. The well-educated upper middle class blacks may be seen as rejecting their origins or otherwise deliberately distancing themselves from their community, and thereby forfeiting their trust and their candor.

A principal challenge confronting the nonminority moderator is the differences in language or dialect, even when group members speak English. Every ethnic community shares linguistic conventions designed to express affiliation with that community and exclude nonmembers. Professional and occupational groups also develop linguistic codes that distance them from outsiders. If the moderators do not understand these linguistic conventions—the special words and phrases unique to that community—they will be handicapped in guiding a discussion. Even if they are familiar with the jargon, there is some question as to whether or not they should use it. Use of "street" or barrio English by a white Anglo moderator may be perceived by participants as patronizing, foolish, and potentially offensive.

Experience and skill should be the major determinants of moderator selection rather than race or ethnicity. If, however, the research issue focuses on products that are used primarily by minority groups or on interracial sensitivities or conflict, selection of a minority moderator is prudent.

MODERATOR RECRUITMENT AND TRAINING

The subject of moderator training raises two important issues. First, how can those who recruit and train moderators identify candidates with the right kind of formal education and the right intellectual skills? Second, what is needed to convert a promising trainee into a perceptive, insightful moderator?

With regard to the first question, the principal attribute we seek in a prospective moderator and analyst is superior intellect. While training can do much to develop inherent talent, it cannot substitute for deficiencies in native intelligence. Conversely, superb moderators have emerged from inadequate training environments by exploiting their intellectual ability.

A good moderator must also be personally interested in and challenged by the study of human motivation and behavior. Conducting qualitative studies requires a natural curiosity about what prompts people to feel and behave as they do. Those who enjoy intellectual discovery and have learned how to pursue it are better equipped to perform qualitative research and to do it well.

Excellent moderators have been drawn from a wide variety of educational disciplines and degree types, including bachelors and postgraduate degrees. Personal characteristics are often more relevant predictors of moderator success than the type or amount of formal education. Nevertheless, we believe that some educational programs optimize the likelihood of success. These prejudices (without convincing quantitative data, that is how they must be regarded) reflect our own experience in selecting and training moderators.

Those with a graduate education in the behavioral sciences and liberal arts generally seem easier to train and more likely to emerge from the training process as skilled group depth interviewers. In the behavioral sciences, psychologists (e.g., social, developmental, or clinical) as well as sociologists bring with them a grasp of human motivation, a sensitivity to interpersonal communication, and an alertness to broad social trends which all aid their moderating efforts. Clinical psychologists, in particular, seem more patient in groups and better able to listen to what group members are saying. Clinical training has made them more aware of their own motives and the role they play in moderating, and more adroit in dealing with destructive participants. Clinicians who have personally received or provided psychotherapy (preferably both) are likely to be especially sensitive to the interpersonal dynamics of the group and most skilled at managing them.

Analysis and report writing, while they draw on training in the social sciences, also appear to benefit from educational programs in philosophy, communications, English, and journalism. Moderators trained in these areas may be better equipped to produce clear, intellectually disciplined, stylishly written qualitative reports.

The physical and mathematical sciences often produce graduates who seem uncomfortable with the soft and speculative results of group interviews. By force of intellectual habit and training, they struggle to extract harder, more quantifiable data from qualitative research than the methodology will support. It is not uncommon for students of the physical sciences to flee group interviewing for the relative "safety in numbers" of cross-tabular data and multivariate analysis.

Anyone who has ever recruited candidates for moderator training has anguished over the relevance of a graduate degree: Does a Ph.D. enhance the likelihood of success as a moderator? Again, while acknowledging that there are many very able moderators with less advanced degrees, and that personality and intellect should be given more weight than education, we prefer to recruit those who have completed a doctoral program. Someone who devotes the years required to obtain a doctorate usually possesses the sort of disciplined intellectual curiosity necessary for good moderating, and emerges with the kind of analytical training that helps them interpret complex motivations and behavior patterns.

In studies dealing with specialized subject matter, training in those technical areas may be more useful than the generalized benefits of a doctoral education. That sort of specialized experience is, however, difficult to acquire and maintain amid the diverse demands of a general market research practice, and we seldom see such individuals broaden into generally able moderators.

It has always seemed to us that selection of promising moderator candidates is more difficult than hiring people for other kinds of skilled professional jobs. Training them has proven equally challenging because no two group interviews are precisely alike and that variety makes the training curriculum almost boundless. Moreover, once trainees have advanced to "solo flight," they are required to produce relevant, actionable data. Unlike reports, group sessions cannot be edited or rescripted after the fact.

Assuming that the trainer starts out with a socially mature, highly motivated candidate who has had no moderating experience but an appropriate educational background, the training program should consist of the following phases:

Phase 1: Orientation

It is common for beginning moderators (or any fledging market researcher) to begin the training with some critical gaps in their education and experience. Behavioral scientists have seldom been exposed to relevant marketing principles; business school graduates may have little or no training in the behavioral sciences. Marketing research is an interdisciplinary profession, and successful practitioners must compensate for gaps in their formal education with on-the-job training.

Those with only a primitive understanding of marketing will require some time to read basic texts and selected articles from the marketing literature. This should be done in addition to pursuing some formal education (for example, in evening marketing courses offered by local universities). Without a grasp of at least the basic principles of marketing, the trainee will fail to understand what is relevant or actionable.

Conversely, those already trained in marketing will require a basic education in psychodynamics. Again, the behavioral science literature provides ample introduction to fundamental principles through texts on nondirective therapy, group therapy, synectics, social behavior, among others.

At the same time that he or she is being introduced to relevant literature, the trainee should be required to observe experienced moderators conduct a wide variety of group interviews. This training is designed principally to expose beginners to the management challenges that are presented in group interviews and the fundamentals of the group process.

Phase 2: Tape Analysis and Report Writing

Perhaps the most useful component of any moderator training program is the experience gained from analyzing the audio recordings of groups conducted by an experienced moderator. There are several reasons for this. First, listening to tapes provides an opportunity to internalize such routines as the introduction, subject transition and general pacing. Second, tape analysis conveys in the most effective way possible how an experienced moderator copes with the many group management problems presented by participants. By the time a trainee has analyzed 60 to 100 group interviews, he or she will have encountered many participant types and will have heard an experienced moderator deal with them in a range of group settings.

Third, and perhaps most important, tape analysis requires a trainee to reduce the apparent conversational chaos of a group interview into its conceptual components so that they can then be integrated into an intellectually disciplined report. In this way, the trainee learns what is relevant, what is important to probe and how to allocate time among the issues to be addressed.

Phase 3: Formal Lectures and Seminars

There are some basic principles that can be conveyed in formal lectures, although what *not* to do in conducting groups is easier to communicate than what to do. Cautions against asking leading questions and intimidating or exploiting participants, for example, can sensitize trainees to these risks. Similarly, research design, group procedures (such as recording, feeding and paying participants), and participant roles or types can all be presented in lecture form.

Handling unanticipated group management problems, however, is best taught in seminar fashion after the trainee has had extensive experience with tape analysis. One useful approach is to play the recording of a trainee's group interview for all of the seminar participants. It is interrupted whenever a participant wishes to ask a question about technique or when the seminar leader wants to illustrate a point or present some technique options for discussion. In this manner, it may require many hours and several seminar sessions to complete one tape. Alternatively, sections of several different tapes may be selected to illustrate particularly interesting technical challenges.

Phase 4: Supervised Moderating

It is difficult to know when the trainee is ready to conduct a group on his or her own. The supervisor has competing obligations: to provide an opportunity for solo moderating as soon as the trainee is ready and, even more important, to assure the client of a professionally competent job.

These conflicting needs can be met in several ways. The trainee can be asked to conduct several groups funded by his or her own agency for training purposes. As an alternative, the trainee can share moderating responsibilities with the supervisor and be given progressively greater freedom in directing the group as his or her skills develop. In this way, their professional inexperience and limitations do not jeopardize the success and value of the group. Meticulous observation and discussion of the trainees' strengths and weaknesses under fire can do much to prepare them for subsequent groups.

Guidelines for Observing Groups

Chapter 15

One of the features which gives groups their enormous power and credibility is the opportunity they afford clients to observe the research as spectators, and even to participate as coaches. The one-way mirror lets clients view their market firsthand without the oblique barrier of large surveys. Client viewing represents something of an evolutionary trend in marketing research. About 15 years ago, perhaps half of all the groups we conducted were attended by clients. Today, it is rare to conduct a qualitative study without having observers present at some or all of the groups.

In general, this trend has been very good for marketing research and those it serves. It reflects greater interest in the process and produces a greater sense of investment in the data, an increased willingness to commission and actually use marketing research, and a better understanding among clients of the strengths and limitations of qualitative techniques. An educated, involved consumer of research is usually a more committed one. In addition, the presence of clients in the viewing room can enhance the process by allowing moderator and viewers to make joint decisions about what issues to pursue more aggressively or abandon, and how to revise priorities as successive groups are conducted. This process is and should be a fluid one; the dynamism and flexibility of groups are two of their great virtues.

Along with these benefits, however, have come certain drawbacks. Viewing can transmute and sometimes distort the outcome if the client and moderator cannot arrive at a comfortable understanding of what their respective roles ought to be and how priorities should be assigned. To explain the kinds of conflicts which can arise, it is important to recognize that a single group exists in two simultaneous forms because it addresses two different, occasionally competing, agendae. The moderator's goal is to collect all the information needed for a complete record and a thorough analysis later on. However, a group viewed by clients meets those *viewers'* needs best when they are able to grasp as much as possible while the interview unfolds. The viewers' group exists principally in "real time" and is often evaluated according to (1) how well viewers understand and follow all the proceedings, (2) how much they enjoy the session, and (3) how clearly they believe the data have emerged without benefit of a later, more leisurely and deliberate analysis.

Conflicts can and do arise when the needs of only one party have been met successfully. These are typically situations in which the client leaves the groups feeling them to be unsatisfactory or incomplete while the moderator is convinced that he or she has everything needed for a complete analysis. There are also situations, however, in which a client has witnessed what seems to be an outstanding group performance yet the moderator is uneasy with the outcome.

Increasing this potential for conflict is the fact that not all clients have a sound theoretical understanding of qualitative techniques or share with the moderator a common set of standards and expectations. Yet enthusiasm and past experience as group spectators may convince viewers that, like ardent fans at a sporting event, they can and should coach energetically from the bleachers. Both clients and moderators must be sensitive to some of the difficulties that can arise when their priorities and standards appear to be different.

We have already argued, for example, that one key test of a successful group interview is the presence of respondent interaction. If none occurs, the process becomes a serial rather than group interview and one crucial benefit of the methodology is lost. Clients, however, often prefer less interactive groups. They are easier to follow since no one talks out of turn, interrupts or answers unasked questions. In addition, interactive interviews tend to be less orderly in their progression through the material, and that apparent disorganization can be difficult to tolerate if the viewer has a rigid topic agenda in mind. Spontaneous interruptions, conversational segues, laughter and other signs that a group has achieved cohesion are essential to group process, but they may leave the spectator ill at ease or confused. Clients who intuitively see the groups as performances rather than processes will be particularly anxious about a possible loss of control. Perhaps, even more common, are boring groups that have little entertainment value but may provide important insights. In either case, clients may be disappointed with the viewing experience even though there is rich raw material for analysis.

When changing or terminating areas of inquiry, one of the most difficult and ambivalent moments for a moderator is opting to close off a topic he or she believes has been explored fully even when there is some suspicion that the clients behind the mirror may not have had their fill. The opposite can also occur, leaving clients bored and frustrated because the moderator seems to be wasting limited time on a subject that was pursued to their satisfaction.

The conflict here, of course, reflects competing priorities: Is the goal of a group interview to demonstrate information to the client or merely to obtain it on his or her behalf? We would argue that the second is more important but we must also acknowledge that qualitative research draws much credibility and popularity from its ability to do the first.

Another source of disappointment may be the unequal participation of various participants, particularly if one expects a well-balanced conversation among vocal contributors. Observers are generally aware that a dominant respondent, if unchecked, can sway or overwhelm a group. However, because most observers do not fully understand the role group leaders play or the ways in which the moderator and analyst may curtail or discount their influence, they sometimes take this concern too seriously. It is the responsibility of the moderator to utilize group leaders to serve their ends (to mimic the natural environment in which some are "more equal" or more dominant than others) and to that extent, active suppression is not always desirable. Live observers, however, become more acutely aware (than tape listeners) of who speaks and how often, and they may urge the moderator to pursue nonparticipants more aggressively or give equal time to everyone in a way that ultimately constrains rather than promotes the research objectives.

There are many other opportunities for conflict, and where they arise, the moderator's burden is to reconcile his or her own standards of technical excellence with the immediate needs and expectations of an audience. Many problems may be forestalled if the moderator explains to new clients in advance how he or she approaches the task and why. When conflicts do arise, however, every moderator must seek an appropriate balance between diplomacy, accommodation, and professional judgment.

Since so many clients choose to observe groups through one-way mirrors, and since their comments and reactions, whether subtly or explicitly conveyed, can have a significant impact on the moderator's handling of groups, it is important that they learn how to observe groups effectively and how to communicate feedback to the moderator. An *educated* observer will have a more satisfactory listening experience and be better able to guide a series of groups to a productive outcome.

MODERATOR FLEXIBILITY

The moderator must be allowed some flexibility in handling the groups. Most observers, especially those with years of listening experience, tend to come to groups with expectations about how they should be handled and what the moderator ought to be doing at any given moment. Observers should remember, however, that an infinite number of patterns and sequences can yield the same basic analytic outcome. There is no single right way to run a group. Observers should not panic, therefore, if the moderator appears to be abandoning a line of questioning momentarily or prioritizing follow-ups and probes in an unexpected sequence. Group interviews are not scripted performances and cannot be evaluated based on their fidelity to the topic outline sequence or a "correct" flow of questions.

UNPRODUCTIVE "DOWN TIME"

Observers should expect "down time" and unproductive moments. They should also be prepared for moments of painful quiet, seemingly aimless discussion, and some excursions off the point. In general, it is the moderator's goal and responsibility to keep the session as productive as possible but few groups, no matter how they are handled, will be consistently informative and lively for a full two hours. Respondents may sometimes need to squirm in anguished silence for a while before yielding up a useful insight.

As was noted earlier, observers should also bear in mind that some lines of questioning which may strike them as initially unproductive can actually produce important insights. Not all the momentous answers or conclusions can be traced to obvious, bellwether questions (such as "what is your principal reason for buying the product?") Sometimes key conclusions are based on a painstaking analysis of several oblique and subtle lines of questioning. In any case, every group is sure to have its dull moments, and weary spectators are urged to be tolerant. Groups may be entertaining but that is an incidental benefit, not an objective.

RESPONDENT RETICENCE

Observers should not assume that tepid or equivocal responses from respondents necessarily mean that they are "holding back." Clients eager for a clear and unambiguous reading of their concepts may interpret retinence or passivity as a signal that respondents are somehow withholding information or failing to be candid. Many concepts do not elicit clear acceptance or rejection because they are neither bad enough nor good enough, neither significant nor relevant enough, to justify more than a murmur of equivocation. This is particularly true in cases where no prototypes or test products are available for sampling. Under those circumstances, retinence is often an indicator of genuine uncertainty or concept irrelevance. Clients who emerge from such groups with the concern that they "just can't get a good reading" on consumer reactions are sometimes expecting an unrealistic level of response or commitment on issues which, in the larger scheme of themes, may be irrelevant to consumers.

RESPONDENTS' PERSONAL FLAWS

Respondents' personal flaws or idiosyncracies must not be permitted to detract from the value of their contributions. It takes all kinds to make meaningful groups and not all participants are bright, entertaining, articulate or even responsive. They are, however, representative of the marketplace and their views must be patiently solicited. The temptation to value the insights of likeable respondents and to dismiss the contributions of unpleasant or dull ones is often overwhelming. Moderators, analysts and observers must all continually resist that impulse if they are to reap the benefits of qualitative research.

RESPONDENT LEADERSHIP AND DOMINANCE

Observers must not assume that dominant personalities necessarily distort the outcome of the group or the analysis. As we noted earlier, hierarchical integration is a goal, not a peril, of the group process and some assertion of leadership and dominance is to be expected, indeed desired, in every group. Observers should not, therefore, assume that a good group is one in which every respondent has had more or less equal time and equal say. Observers should bear in mind, too, that individuals who are subject to persuasion by dominant personalities in a group setting are equally vulnerable to similar persuasion in other environments. Neither sales reps nor advertisements will ever have direct access to such individuals without competition from other points of view or sources of influence.

OBSERVER–MODERATOR INTERACTION

Observers should not disrupt the session with frequent notes or communications to the moderator. Observers often wish to alert the moderator to lingering questions or areas of interest they wish to have probed before the close of the group. Since intermittent notes are distracting to the moderator and disruptive to the group, it is generally preferable to jot down questions or issues as they come to mind and send (or bring) the list in shortly before the close of the group. Most moderators signal thay they are about to terminate so that a message can be relayed or others may excuse themselves and come briefly to the viewing room for final instructions. Observers often find that many of the questions they jot down are eventually addressed to their satisfaction by the close of the group and those that are not can be readily reopened by a skilled moderator. In years past, some moderators were requested to wear earphones for the purpose of receiving client direction but it is a procedure most moderators find intolerable and has been largely abandoned.

One final caution: Questions or suggestions sent to the moderator should be clear and concise. A moderator must be able to grasp their essence quickly without halting the group. An unclear (or undecipherable) question will require that the moderator puzzle over its meaning, leave the room for clarification or simply ignore the question. None of those alternatives is desirable.

In addition, directions for issues or areas to emphasize should reflect a consensus among observers about the study goals. On several occasions, suggestions for reemphasis or redirection sent from the viewing room did *not* reflect complete agreement among all the observers and the result was a group that complied with one person's directive but violated the needs of everyone else.

PREMATURE CONCLUSIONS

Observers should resist jumping to firm conclusions without a formal analysis. An instinctive drive for closure tempts clients and moderators to emerge from initial groups with a set of conclusions or hypotheses, and indeed, this process of continually building and modifying on-the-spot interpretations is useful in guiding the evolution of a group project. Immediate debriefings are useful. Groups should not, however, be expected to provide clear and easy direction under live conditions. Observers must be prepared for some ambiguity and contradiction because group outcomes are seldom clearcut. The burden of final interpretation rightfully falls on those who analyze the recordings.

Analyzing the Groups

Chapter 16

Although client spectators are frequently present at group interviews and may even be prepared to take initial action on the basis of immediate or "topline" results, careful and deliberate analysis remains crucial to sound qualitative research. Just as the power and validity of that analysis are contingent on well-run groups, so does the value of the groups depend ultimately on skill and depth of interpretation.

It is the moderator's responsibility to prospect for raw materials, and to do that, he or she must be able to recognize important revelations and distinguish meaningful insights from camouflage or superficiality. Ultimately, however, it is the responsibility of the analyst to mine those raw materials at their deepest levels. This activity cannot be completed while the group is underway. It requires time, close attention, and unlimited access to a verbatim recording of the session.

WHO DOES THE ANALYSIS?

We have been discussing the moderator and analyst as if they were two separate entities, not only because these roles are distinct in time but also because they may actually be assumed by two different people working closely together. Some qualitative specialists have argued that only the moderator or some other firsthand observer can provide a thorough analysis of group sessions because observers see the facial expressions and other nonverbal cues that qualify spoken comments. it can even be difficult for a listener who was not present at the group to identify speakers and recognize continuity in their remarks.

There is no doubt that information available to an observer can add an important dimension to the analysis, especially these latent meanings that speech may actually camouflage or contradict. Sometimes, however, client schedules require that someone other than the moderator review tapes. Under those circumstances what can be done to ensure a complete and penetrating analysis?

First, it is our belief that the moderator can assist people who may be listening to the tapes by mentioning aloud in the group nonverbal gestures of assent of disagreement which would not otherwise be captured in a tape recording. Comments like, "I see you nodding your head, Anne," or "You seem to be frowning, Sam," relay important information to those not present while also serving to provoke more detailed verbal responses during the group.

Equally important, the moderator must communicate personal impressions and conclusions to the analyst and then review the report to confirm its accuracy and completeness. Thus, every report should represent a close collaboration between moderator and analyst, in which both individuals test and enrich conclusions drawn by the other.

HOW SHOULD NOTES BE TAKEN?

A sound analysis requires not only careful listening but also careful and well-organized note taking. Proceeding directly from tape listening to report writing without that intermediate step, even when there is only one group to analyze, is an act of recklessness that can seriously jeopardize the final product.

Note-taking styles are a matter of personal preference and work habit, neither of which we would presume to dictate. There are, however, some basic pointers and techniques to keep in mind.

1. *The analysis should be started as soon after the groups are completed as schedule allows.* Memory begins to erode quickly, and even if the moderator is not personally analyzing the tapes, he or she will make some contribution on the basis of recollections.

2. *The analyst should always have at hand the screening criteria and stimulus materials used in the groups.* Even the moderator may forget eligibility requirements or positioning platforms in a matter of days.

3. *Groups should be analyzed in a sequence that allows the analyst to compare*

relevant segments for sharper contrast. The analyst might, for example, want to play a group or two of users before proceeding to nonusers, or a group of women and then men.

4. *It is helpful in taking notes to identify relevant topic areas, especially those likely to become topic headings in the report (for example, current usage patterns, brand images, or unmet needs).* If additional material on a given topic emerges later in the discussion, it can be placed under its proper heading and integrated into the analysis. Some analysts like to color code group notes so that they can readily identify the session from which a comment was taken. At the same time, they may also choose to organize notes by subject matter rather than by group to facilitate a comprehensive (cross-sectional) view of each topic rather than a group-by-group focus. It also makes material easier to find and access when writing the report. We favor this cross-sectional, subject-oriented analysis, despite its greater difficulty.

5. *The analyst should save space in the notes for personal interpretations and hypotheses.* It is important to record not only what respondents claim to do or feel but also, the analyst's own impressions of what those feelings and behaviors mean and whether or not they seem credible.

6. *The analyst must organize observations so that product reactions can be linked to the reasons or motivations that seem to drive them.* It is important that the notes capture not just discrete responses but whole worldviews—the way participants conceptualize a product area rather than merely how they seem to "vote."

7. *The analyst must not overlook or avoid recording fairly obvious or mundane information about product usage or image.* Similarly, the analyst must note unimaginative or routine responses as well as the creative and unusual ones. In a qualitative analysis, we welcome stunning insights and surprises but we also require basic background information as a context in which to evaluate them.

8. *The analyst should never ignore the lone dissenting voice in an effort to capture the gist of group opinion.* That single individual may very well represent an important market segment and his or her views should be available for inclusion in the report.

HOW SHOULD THE DATA BE ANALYZED?

Qualitative analysis always begins during the group session itself since the moderator must remain continually alert to analytic implications if the group is to be guided successfully. For example, the moderator must decide which issues warrant elaboration and which may be abandoned; he or she must note that a participant has contradicted earlier statements and decide how that inconsistency should be pursued.

This spontaneous analysis which actually shapes the group outcome is what makes group moderating so challenging. The moderator must be scrupulously attentive to the meaning of the proceedings in order to manage and direct them. For that reason, it is difficult to separate the principles of group analysis from the list of moderating techniques already laid out in previous chapters. In most cases, however, they bear repeating.

1. *The analyst, like the moderator, must be attentive to the order in which respondents raise issues and the length of time they choose to spend on them.* On the other hand, not all of the issues respondents choose to ignore are insignificant. Indeed, there are times in which the absence of discussion is more telling than its presence. Clear evidence that respondents are squirming in silent discomfort or hostile avoidance at the mention of a subject should alert us to its repressed significance. The paradoxical idea that *either* presence or absence of discussion can betray the significance of a subject attests to the difficulties of qualitative analysis. There is no clear set of rules to which one can turn for unambiguous interpretations. In the following illustration, the relative insignificance of price as a determinant of shampoo selection was reflected in the absence of any discussion on that point. Note that the analyst's job is facilitated by a moderator who tests hypotheses and interpretations in the group by exposing them for rejection or validation by group members.

(At 1 hour 40 minutes)

MODERATOR: I notice that although we have been discussing how you go about selecting shampoos there has been no discussion at all about what they cost. Does that mean it is not an important consideration?

RESPONDENT #1: Well, all the really good ones are roughly the same price and I'm not going to sacrifice the way my hair looks and feels for a dollar or two.

RESPONDENT #2: You can really injure your hair by using bargain shampoos—drying out, split ends—things like that.

By contrast, in the following example from a group of physicians discussing antiarthritis drugs, physicians' failure to discuss efficacy without prompting, actually signaled its acknowledged importance.

(At 1 hour 15 minutes)

MODERATOR: We've been talking about side-effects, samples, habit, price and many other factors that may guide your selection of an antiinflammatory, but there has been little mention of efficacy—does it work? That suggests to me that efficacy, in antiinflammatories at least, is less important to you than these other factors.

PHYSICIAN #1: Oh no! Not at all. It's just that we all assume that efficacy is more important. You don't have to say what's so obvious.

PHYSICIAN #2: That's right! And also what product will work for a particular patient is unpredictable. So you may have to try them in sequence to see what is best for the patient. Efficacy *is* important but there are no generalizations. There's not much to say about it.

2. *The analyst must look for clues to the intensity of people's reactions.* Frequently, what is more important than consensus or diversity of opinion is intensity of people's feelings and the reasoning or justification offered in support of them. Survey research is uniquely suited to head counts; qualitative research is uniquely suited to motivational analysis. Thus, it is important in writing the report to communicate not only the degree of consensus, but also the strength or conviction with which views appear to be held. The presence of a small segment of hostile and intractible rejectors will have different implications than a small segment of disinterested or apathetic rejectors.

One of the ways in which people communicate the strength of their feelings is by stating them in forceful unambiguous terms, for example, "I hate that cake mix." Another is by repeating them consistently in response to several different (or differently worded) questions. Sometimes, however, participants may communicate enthusiasm or rejection in other less direct ways. A physician who suggested laughingly that the information produced by a device belonged in *The Journal of Continuous Patient Monitoring* was communicating rather strongly, through derisive humor, that he saw the product as entirely trivial and irrelevant.

3. *The analyst must be attentive to the reasons people give for acceptance or rejection.* These accounts help us to determine whether the product can overcome its handicaps or capitalize on its virtues. Respondents who refuse to buy a power tool because they are "afraid that it is too difficult to handle" are telling us something very different from those who believe the tool does not meet any of their needs. Such cases illustrate the extent to which motivations rather than numbers often hold the key to successful marketing, if by marketing we mean lifting the barriers to product purchase and finding the triggers to propel it.

Although people cannot always explain why they feel the way they do about a product, their language—particularly the analogies they use in describing product reactions—can contain important clues to the nature of their approval or rejection. A participant who is unable to explain why he dislikes a creamy spread but offhandedly compares it to toothpaste in a tube, is communicating something important about its perceived inedibility and perhaps artificiality. More literal phrasing would not necessarily capture that imagery so vividly or so well.

4. *The analyst should be prepared to doubt or disbelieve some of what is said.* Since the distinctive value of qualitative research lies in its depth of analysis and its commitment to uncovering latent meanings, someone charged with analyzing qualitative data is frequently faced with the dilemma of when to take respondent's comments at face value and when to distrust them. Clients faced with several groups of respondents who have roundly criticized an ad or product concept often ask whether that negativity is a true index of feeling or a predictor of future behavior. Conversely, choruses of praise

and earnest pledges to purchase are sometimes mistrusted by the marketer about to invest substantial sums in product development.

This problem, common to all research methodologies, reflects two basic sources of error. Respondents may not choose to tell us the truth or they may not recognize it themselves. Qualitative research gives us a unique opportunity to distinguish what is said from what is actually meant—which brings us to the question of how this is done.

Qualitative studies, unlike surveys, permit us to frame and reframe questions in ways that test the strength and conditions of a "yes" or "no" verdict. In listening to these explanations, the analyst should be attentive to the cues which suggest some discrepancy between what has been said and what may actually be true.

Self-contradiction

It is not uncommon for respondents to make remarks during the course of the session which appear inconsistent, and a good analyst is always on the lookout for signals which contradict what respondents have stated explicitly. While the analyst should never dismiss the possibility of midstream conversion, self-contradiction often hints at an unresolved conflict. In the following illustration, a physician begins describing his response to a device concept by telling the moderator that he would never try a product unless it had first seen five years' experience abroad:

DOCTOR: Medicine is too litigious. No way I'm going to try a new model from a new company until they've used it in Europe with no problems for at least five years.

Later, that same respondent, whose current conservative behavior seemed consistent with his cautious viewpoints, surprised the group by declaring his intent to use it.

DOCTOR: I would use it. It seems better than the others that are available.
MODERATOR: But, you haven't used other [similar] models yet? Why this one?
DOCTOR: Well, this one's a little better than those. It might not have some of the problems. I would try it anyway.

In the context of previous comments and a reported style of practice which suggested slow adoption rather than experimentation, it seemed more reasonable to conclude that interest in the concept represented social acquiescence rather than genuine commitment. His voice had previously been strong but was now more subdued. His reticent physical demeanor communicated discomfort and embarrassment at being one of the less experienced in the group and uneasiness at his own discernible inconsistency.

In another session, a consumer gave similarly mixed signals in talking about a convenience cooking product she was asked to evaluate. She had been recruited as an individual who prepared meals and baked "from scratch" but after subsequent probing acknowledged occasional uses of convenience products.

(At ½ hour into the discussion)
RESPONDENT: I never bother with cake mixes and things like that. They never taste as good. And I don't enjoy it. I'd rather work a little harder and know it's really fresh. You know? My family appreciates that.

Later in the session, more ambiguous signals were sent.

(At 1½ hours into the session)
MODERATOR: Well what kind of experience have you actually had with these products?
RESPONDENT: Oh, some. If I'm desperate, you know. It's not like I never used mixes. It's a job. You know. I feel, I don't know, a little guilty. I'm not out there working, it's the least I can do.

This respondent subsequently rejected the product, but a review of her cumulative comments suggested that rejection might be more theoretical or philosophical than real and that, indeed, if the product could be positioned so as to overcome her sense of guilt about short cuts, she might actually use it.

Socially Correct Responses

While market researchers are ultimately dependent on what respondents choose to tell them and there is no simple or reliable test of truthfulness, it is generally prudent to treat socially acceptable responses with greater caution than answers which appear to offer a risky or unconventional disclosure. A skilled moderator does his or her best to create a tolerant, nonjudgmental atmosphere that minimizes respondents' sense of vulnerability and encourages some risk taking. Thus, clients often find that potential customers are more diplomatic when discussing products in sales meetings and conventions (where client identity is disclosed) than they are in groups, where the mirror acts as a social buffer and the moderator has taken pains to promote candor. It is safe to assume, however, that even in a candid group environment, respondents do not necessarily speak the truth, even if they are not intentionally lying.

A comparison of how respondents describe themselves in the screening phase and how they describe themselves in the group under more intense probing reminds us that people often position themselves on the basis of how they want or need to be seen by themselves and others. As a result, we have found groups of self-reported "aspirin-avoiders" who, on close questioning, behave remarkably like "aspirin-users." A review of the mixed signals they send may not necessarily produce accurate predictions of product acceptance or rejection, but they do sensitize us to important sources of ambivalence which can help us to make products less threatening or damaging to consumer self-image.

One difficulty in spotting the socially acceptable response is the fact that groups, like any microcosm, often develop their own norms and conventions. These may, on occasion, deviate from the conventions of broader society, where people are generally rewarded for nonconfrontation and social conformity. Indeed, exaggerated and contentious behavior can become not just acceptable but mandatory, if an aggressive climate has developed during the session and the moderator has not successfully diffused it. Under those (unusual) circumstances, nonconformity and gratuitous hostility can be established as comfortable norms.

The question we must always ask, therefore, is: What kind of behavior did a particular group seem to be tolerating and rewarding? While we often worry about social acquiescence and yea saying, the opposite phenomenon sometimes occurs as well. Participants may reject concepts they might actually have embraced under other circumstances. One or two vocal individuals with a rebellious or strident point of view can provoke entire groups into expressing a diffuse social hostility (that is, antiadvertising, anticommercialism, antitechnology) directed specifically toward a product or idea. It is the moderator's job to blunt those reactions, of course, but the analyst must always be sensitive to the possibility that even in a skillfully run group, not all negative comments are trustworthy and not all hostility is candor.

Some cues suggesting the possibility that an individual's response (positive or negative) was socially motivated include:

- Simple responses ("Yes, I like it" or "No, I don't") offered in response to probes but seldom volunteered.
- Responses which suggest either hostility or personal allegiance ("I've already said it twice . . ." or "You've sold me").
- Responses which seem to reflect anxiety (weak voice, hesitation, among others).
- Respondents' inability to restate reasons for acceptance or rejection ("For the same reason" and "It's like I said").
- Responses which seem to contradict earlier statements of philosophy or behavior.

5. *The analyst should focus on market segments, not individuals or groups.* Because the goal in qualitative analysis is generalization, individual group members should be singled out only as examples or illustrations of more general behaviors and attitudes. The analyst should not dwell on idiosyn-

cratic case studies or participant profiles as ends in themselves, regardless of how interesting those may be. If we cannot generalize from qualitative data (and note, we say *generalize* rather than draw statistical inferences) the analysis is of no value to the marketer who is about to make far-reaching decisions, or to the questionnaire designer who must focus on issues that are potentially generalizable and actionable.

If the individual participant is not the unit of analysis, then who or what is? Is it each group of seven or ten participants, or something else? Certainly, different group sessions conducted within the same study often do exhibit such sharply contrasting identities that there is strong temptation to maintain those distinctions in the written analysis. Generally speaking, however, extensive comparison of group sessions should be avoided because the group is a temporary vehicle for eliciting information and not a permanent unit of analysis. While groups recruited for specific characteristics (such as awareness levels, purchase behavior, demographics or region) may indeed exhibit pertinent differences, it is preferable, in those instances, to think and talk about *market segments* rather than groups per se, since each group is a temporary social unit that dissolves at the end of two hours.

Discernible attitude and behavior differences will often emerge *within* groups, and these differences are an important focus of analysis. An important goal of marketing is, after all, to identify and define segments. No population can be well understood or reached as a diffuse and undifferentiated mass of individuals. An important goal of qualitative research is, therefore, to identify and compare attitude segments. Note that by segments, we generally mean population groups with different product orientation. In order to identify segments of people with similar outlooks, the analyst should pay careful attention to a respondent's opinion *patterns* and not just responses to specific questions.

Writing
the Report

Chapter 17

Since the ultimate product of a group interview study is most often a written report (and since many key decision makers may never be exposed to the groups in any other way), the report should be as sound as the research that it describes. Informal memos and "topline" documents may be structured as the situation and the client requires, but we believe there are some basic requirements that every formal qualitative report should meet if it is to be considered a complete document. This chapter offers some guidelines.

THE ROLE OF A QUALITATIVE REPORT

While reports almost always play a pivotal role in guiding the use of market research data, they play an especially important role in qualitative research because there is no shorthand access to the data. The purchaser of survey data has recourse to computer tables which, even without benefit of formal analysis, offer an efficient and useful summary of the findings. The data can be assembled in a statistical record that lends itself more readily to direct and unambiguous interpretation than a tape or transcript.

In qualitative research, there is no intermediate step between group proceedings (or the taped record of those) and the analytical interpretation. Thus, in any qualitative analysis, much of the power and the validity lie in the telling—that is in the selection, organization, and even the phrasing of interpretative materials. There are many different styles of report presentation and we do not offer any one format as the only legitimate option. The author of a report may choose to state conclusions up front or at the end; to quote people liberally or infrequently; and to call them "participants," "respondents," "consumers" or whatever else they choose. Issues like those are a matter of personal or professional preference and do not necessarily have bearing on the validity of the report.

In our view, the ideal qualitative report lies somewhere between good science and good journalism: carefully structured and precisely, but gracefully, written. Many writers manage to strike a satisfactory balance between intellectual rigor and literary elegance. When, however, that lofty ideal cannot be met, a qualitative report should, at the very least, be logically organized and easy to read.

THE GOALS OF A QUALITATIVE REPORT

In order to understand what is required in a qualitative report, we must first ask what its objectives are. It is probably easiest to answer this deceptively simple question by stating what a qualitative report is not. *It is not, or should not be, a sequential summary or transcript of the group discussion.* It should be a logically organized and coherent interpretation of the meaning of those events. An illustration of the two approaches will help make the point.

Transcript of the Proceedings Approach

The moderator passed around copies of the concept statement and read them aloud with the respondents. Then they were asked what they thought of this new floor cleaning product.

One respondent, who does not like to clean floors, said she felt that the product was too much like what was already available to attract her interest. Another made the comment that she thought it might be worth considering so long as it wasn't too expensive. When asked what she meant by "too expensive" she said that anything costing more than her current floor cleaning product was probably unacceptable. . . .

This approach is inadequate on several accounts. First, it is descriptive rather than analytical, generally focusing on superficial statements of opinion with little attention to underlying meanings or motivations. Second, it relies on temporal sequence rather than logic to structure the organization of material. Although the order in which respondents tackle issues is often a clue to their relevance, the order in which specific respondents make specific statements should not in and of itself determine the flow of sentences in a report.

Finally, a report which summarizes what took place in precisely the order it occurred gives the group session a level of permanent reality and significance it ought not to have. The group session is merely a vehicle for eliciting information rather than a performance to be recaptured. On a practical level, a transcript not only burdens the reader with irrelevant detail, it also diverts attention from the generalizable meaning of the events by focusing on the events themselves.

An improved, conceptually organized version of the same material would read quite differently. Note that in two or three paragraphs, one can capture and make explicit what lies dormant in several tedious pages of descriptive (or transcriptive) prose.

Conceptual Approach

Reactions to the concept appear to depend principally on consumers' personal orientation to flooring maintenance. One segment, who might be described as compulsive cleaners, are prepared to commit significant amounts of energy and expense to floor care because they believe that a clean house is an important reflection on them and that the most demanding test of home hygiene is the status of their floors. These women may have new floors they wish to protect against deterioration or older floors they work hard to restore. In all cases, however, they seem prepared to pay a price premium for any technological advantage they can obtain in floor care and look favorably on the new product.

The second approach, which is able to capture and communicate information much more efficiently than the first, transcends individual comments (except as they may illustrate a particular point) and focuses on the global significance of many individual comments. In that way, it synthesizes, structures and interprets data which, if reported as a string of observations, would leave the task of analysis almost entirely to the reader.

ORGANIZING KEY ELEMENTS OF THE REPORT

Rules of logical progression should dictate the structure of a qualitative report much as they govern any other type of nonfiction. It is generally desirable to begin with an introductory chapter that reviews research goals and methodology, then proceed to an analysis of the data (in one or more chapters), and finally to draw the relevant marketing implications and recommendations in an ending chapter. Some authors attach marketing recommendations in the front for easy access. It is also customary to provide an "Executive Summary" in the front of the report for readers who wish to learn the gist of the findings quickly without necessarily reading a detailed analysis.

1. *Introduction*

The goal of an introductory chapter is to acquaint the reader with the research objectives, the methodological approach, and any special conditions or procedures that should be taken into consideration in evaluating the outcome. The level of detail required here is a matter both of taste and institutional custom.

We believe it is usually sufficient to state the general purpose of the study and review briefly the areas of inquiry. A detailed topic outline should be reserved for the appendix. By way of illustration:

> This study was undertaken on behalf of *(COMPANY)* to explore motivations and behavior patterns related to soft drink consumption. The project was designed as the first phase of a comprehensive research program to generate hypotheses for quantitative testing and guide questionnaire development.
>
> Specific areas of inquiry included the social, psychological, and physical needs driving soft drink consumption, consumer brand perceptions and allegiance, and current usage paterns . . . .

Even in a study with more focused objectives such as evaluating reactions to an advertising concept, it is helpful to remind the reader that general attitudes and usage patterns were probed as a framework for evaluating concept reactions.

Following the statement of objectives, there should be a description of the methodology. First, the reader should be told how many groups were conducted in which locations and with what kinds of respondents. Any special screening procedures should be noted so that the data can be evaluated in its proper context. Reports are often read by people without first-hand knowledge of the study, and in some cases these reports are consulted months or years later by a new cast of marketers. The report is often the only permanent record of what transpired.

Second, readers should be alerted to any unusual procedures that may have been used (for example, sorting or projective pictures) *and* any *special precautions that were taken to protect the research from bias* (such as rotation of concepts). Group interviews have become so commonplace that it is not generally necessary to define the basic methodology or describe ordinary procedures in a typical report, but any departures from the conventional group interview should be noted.

Finally, every introductory chapter must contain a prominent caveat or caution on generalization which alerts readers to the limitations of the methodology. In particular, readers should be reminded of the inappropriateness of statistical projections based on qualitative research alone. There are many ways to convey this general idea but a paragraph making at least these key points is recommended:

> The reader is cautioned that the findings reported here are qualitative, not quantitative, in nature. The study was designed to explore *how* respondents feel and behave rather than to determine *how many* think or act in specific ways. Therefore, the findings cannot serve as a basis for statistical generalizations, but should instead be viewed as working hypotheses, subject to quantitative validation.

Some authors choose to specify the reasons this caveat should be applied, for example:

> Respondents constitute a small nonrandom sample of relevant consumers and are therefore not statistically representative of the universe from which they have been drawn.

In our view, one need not dwell on the fact that group interview respondents represent a volunteer sample since all respondents are by definition volunteers, whether they are surveyed in their homes or interviewed in a group facility.

2. Analysis of the data

A good qualitative report, like any persuasive analytic document, should be organized and written in a way that leads the reader without resistance or surprise from one set of propositions to the next. The relevant organizing principle is not necessarily the sequence of discussion in the group sessions but rather the logic of the subject matter. The moderator's topic outline may be helpful in that regard but should not be slavishly adhered to if another sequence seems more effective.

Reports that adopt the sequence of the topical outline as the organizing structure may miss the opportunity to present the study results in a more action-oriented manner by focusing, for example, on marketing problems or market segments rather than iterative topics. The organization and order of the topical outline and report may differ precisely because their objectives differ. The topic outline is designed to extract data and the report is intended to conceptualize and interpret it.

It is usually advisable to progress from the general to the more specific so that the reader has a context in which to place narrower observations and findings. Thus, a report on reactions to a new snack concept would most appropriately begin the analysis section with a discussion of general eating or snack orientations, and then progress to brand image and allegiance before actually reporting the response to new concepts.

In evaluating reactions to a product or ad, it is often helpful to organize the information in terms of appeals and barriers, as long as the author is ultimately prepared to weigh them all and draw a set of integrated conclusions. Of course, each subject and each data set have their own innate structure which will tend to dictate the way the information is best organized and unfolded. A routine-type ledger accounting of appeals and barriers may seem tedious and poorly organized if each product feature offers both incentives and disincentives that are inextricably linked. Light weight, for example, may be both a virtue (easy to carry) and a liability (easy to knock over). Under those circumstances, an integrated discussion of the feature and its benefits may be more effective. There are also instances in which the product benefits are obvious and self-defined as with safety caps, and in those cases the focus may may need to be on problems of execution or credibility with only token acknowledgment of appeals.

Whether or not an appeals-and-barriers or pros-and-cons approach has been taken, it is usually desirable to begin or end with a general over-view so that the net assessment can be quickly grasped. It is also important that any minimum requirements or nonnegotiable consumer demands be made explicit. A car phone, for example, may be seen as offering a set of four or five attractive benefits but only if it provides good reception.

3. *Marketing implications*

The role of the marketing conclusions chapter is to outline marketing opportunities and limitations, offer a set of recommendations and suggest directions for future research, where appropriate. It is here that the author must be especially careful never to overlook the ultimate goal of the re-search. A psychoanalytically rich interpretation of personal hygiene and deodorant products is ultimately of little value to the client if it cannot be linked to a set of actionable marketing implications—for example, a posi-tioning which directly reflects consumer motivations or a new product directed at needs not currently addressed. Complex motivational analyses may be fascinating (and in some settings, they are valued ends in them-selves) but in the context of marketing research, their value lies in their ability to guide sound marketing decisions. The author of a qualitative report has responsibility for helping readers draw direct links between the motivational analyses and the marketing implications. General information about the market as well as knowledge of the client's goals and constraints should be reflected in this chapter if the recommendations are to be re-sponsible and complete.

Since a "go or no-go" decision is seldom made solely on the basis of qualitative findings, conclusions and recommendations should be re-strained and conditional. On the other hand, clients often charge that analysts take too tentative and equivocal a position in order to protect themselves from decision-making liabilities or the embarrassment of error.

We sympathize with this client complaint. Reports that waffle and temporize usually command little respect and often leave the client feeling fundamentally unsatisfied. We therefore urge writers to be as forceful as professional integrity and prudence allow. Their responsibility is to indicate where the data may be inadequate while also taking every legitimate opportunity to offer advice.

We recall a client who asked the moderator to phone in with a summary of two groups and then said bluntly, "Now, I have to make a decision—tell me what to do." The moderator protested that a decision was premature and that he couldn't possibly offer a recommendation based on so little information. The client responded by saying, "A decision has to be made immediately. Which do you prefer—that I make it based on no information whatsoever or that I accept a recommendation from someone who has already done two groups?" When it was put to him that way, the moderator felt obliged to offer an opinion, qualifications and doubts notwithstanding.

The following examples of phrasing reflect some caution but do not abdicate responsibility for making recommendations.

- The qualitative findings give reason for optimism about market interest in the new product concept . . . We therefore recommend that the concept be further developed and formal executions be tested.
- While actual market demand may not necessarily meet the test of profitability, the data reported here suggest that there is widespread interest in the new device.
- The results of this study suggest that ad version #3 is most promising because it elicited more enthusiastic responses and because it appears to describe situations under which consumers actually expect to use the product . . .

Some common sins of commission or omission in drawing conclusions include a tendency to (1) merely summarize logical alternatives or state the obvious; (2) state preference without making the marketing consequences explicit, and (3) rest conclusions on unrealistic assumptions about the product concept. These approaches seriously undermine the strength and value of an otherwise sound report.

1. *Summary of logical alternatives*

A common deficiency of qualitative reports, especially those that are written by the novice analyst, is a compilation of logical alternatives rather than an interpetation that contributes to some marketing or research implementation. This naive approach to analysis is reflected in the following illustration from a report on physician evaluation of a new antiarthritic drug.

With regard to anticipated initial use of (the new product), doctors variously claim they would prescribe the product:

- As an equal alternative to all currently available antiarthritics
- As the drug of first choice among the newer class of antiarthritics, i.e. as a replacement for current favorites

- As an equal alternative among current favorites
- For patients with certain health problems, e.g., heart, kidney or liver
- For elderly patients
- For patients on antidiabetics, antihypertensives or digoxin
- As a drug of last choice among newer antiarthritics.

This list of potential uses merely aggregates all of the possible conditions of use and provides little beyond what was conceptually available prior to the study. As a result, the analyst offers here nothing to help order or interpret these responses in a way that guides marketing action.

Conclusions should select for special comment and evaluation particular uses that address a current market need or suggest a market position that distinguishes the concept from other products. At every least, the writer is obliged to array prospective applications in accordance with some inferred user priorities so that the client who commissioned the report can take appropriate action.

In another report on hair care products, a trainee-analyst began the section by observing that:

> If (the concept) proved to be a better shampoo—that is, it cleaned better, did no damage to hair, and was no more expensive than other shampoos, it would most likely be tried.

Although this statement was not inaccurate, product management could probably have drawn this same conclusion without actually conducting a study. Instead, the analyst should have focused on what advantages the product could actually claim and whether they were sufficient to overcome the purchase inertia that sustained dominant brands.

2. *Conclusions that summarize preference without drawing marketing implications*

A manufacturer who was considering changing the status of a prescription product to over-the-counter availability was especially interested in the reaction of pharmacists to that potential marketing strategy. The major conclusion offered by the report stated:

> Pharmacists prefer that (the product) remain a prescription product.

No further elaboration of determinants or consequences of preference was provided. While surely the finding was relevant (and predictable), the principal burden of the report should have been to address why pharmacists felt that way, how intense their feelings were and most important of all, how their preference would be reflected in future behavior. Would they view the company's action as regrettable but inevitable, or would their pique be expressed consciously or otherwise in actions calculated to penalize the client company? Preference alone is an inadequate conclusion in a qualitative report. Marketing consequence—the answer to the ubiquitious "So what?"—is usually the goal of the exploration. Satisfying that objective assures, of course, that the moderator has exposed the data for analysis.

3. *Conclusions resting on unrealistic assumptions*

A conclusion regarding the acceptability of a product or concept is useful and relevant only to the extent that the assessment is made within the context of realistic assumptions about the market environment and the product. The conclusion that "a new appliance will have broad appeal at a price below $30" is irrelevant if the cost of manufacture exceeds that figure. Unless an attribute is explicitly stated in a concept description, assumptions about superior performance (". . . If it has the pain-killing efficacy of narcotics without causing addition") or lower cost are generally unwarranted and market appraisal based on overoptimistic assumptions does a disservice to the client.

It is common for marketing researchers to conclude their final report chapter with a section describing implications for future research, a section often viewed by clients with an appropriate dose of cynicism. The habit is generally cultivated in academia where no study can pretend to be definitive, and it is carried on in consulting professions where, as industry jokes would have it, people perform studies in order to conclude that another study is needed. Our policy is to include such a section only if significant questions remain unanswered and/or where there was some ongoing expectation that the completed study would guide forthcoming research.

When proposing follow-up surveys or further qualitative research, the author should be careful to consider whether the product or issue appears to warrant further expense, since not all qualitative studies require or deserve quantification. One should never feel compelled to suggest a follow-up; neither should one feel embarrassed or self-serving to do so if further research is genuinely warranted.

WRITING STYLE

Organizing and conveying key ideas persuasively requires not only logical thinking but also clear and powerful writing. There is a well-known maxim in journalism: Tell readers what you are about to say; say it; and then afterwards, tell them what you have just said. This formula often makes for tedious reading but the general principle is a sound one. The author is continually responsible for giving the readers their bearings. This is best done with explicit titles and subtitles, clear introductory paragraphs, and a lucid style of writing that propels the reader toward conclusions.

On the subject of style, we can only report our personal biases since, here especially, taste rather than universal standards must reign. Questions which arise frequently include the following:

What Tense?

It is customary in social science research to report data in the present tense. That convention is intended to reflect and reinforce the generalizability of the findings. The data might otherwise appear to represent only one sample population at one point in time.

While group interview analysis is not projectable in the statistical sense, it is (or should be) projectable in a qualitative sense. That is to say, it should reflect the feelings and motivations of some portion of the universe it purports to study rather than a few individual participants. If one cannot properly generalize on the basis of qualitative research, it becomes a tool for clinical case study, and its only value lies in what it tells us about a handful of specific respondents. If one wishes to reinforce the marketing value of qualitative research, it is desirable to acknowledge the broader significance of the analysis by writing in the present tense, for example:

> While beer drinkers often single out a "favorite brand," they also typically report having a set of two or three acceptable brands which they view as nearly interchangeable.

OR

> Do-it-yourselfers commonly explain that while they are motivated in part by potential cost savings, they also experience enormous personal satisfaction and pride in doing jobs at home for which they can take credit. A do-it-yourself orientation is also fueled by the widespread belief, perhaps rationalization, that one simply cannot buy the same level of craftsmanship and commitment from professionals.

There are, however, certain circumstances under which the past tense may be more appropriate, particularly when one wishes to describe reactions which were clearly rooted in the context of the group session and can only be understood within that setting. For example, if we suspect that the particular phrasing of a concept, the order in which it was presented, or other procedural details have affected responses, it is fair and prudent to convey this qualification by writing in the past tense:

> While initial reactions to the concept were generally favorable, there was a gradual erosion of that enthusiasm during the course of discussion as respondents appeared to discover potential drawbacks to the system . . .

Respondents who were presented first with the convenience positioning seemed generally less tolerant of a price premium than those first exposed to the freshness positioning.

OR

Once those considering purchase had an opportunity to question those who were already owned the appliance, there was an evident dampening of interest and optimistic expectations.

It requires a certain linguistic dexterity to shift gracefully from one tense to another in the same report, but when an author wishes to speak specifically about a particular group and to refrain from generalization, the shift is pardonable and perhaps mandatory.

How to Describe Concensus

While recognizing that qualitative research is not statistically projectable, clients generally want groups to provide a rough index of the breadth of market interest or acceptability. Indeed, under some circumstances, no other measure of market appeal is available. One of the great challenges of qualitative report writing is the need to generalize or aggregate responses without appearing to imply a statistical frequency. If all or most respondents have expressed similar reactions, it is desirable to communicate that level of consensus without suggesting that all or most consumers would necessarily share that same view in a projectable market survey.

Conversely, if only one respondent in 9 or in 18 expresses an attitude, it is appropriate to suggest that this viewpoint is probably not widely held. Under these circumstances, report writers might consider the past tense as a way of singling out an idiosyncratic reaction or event whose general significance cannot be assessed, for example:

One respondent indicated that he had heard of the concept before but he could recall only the name and nothing more.

In general, it is wise to cultivate a vocabulary of terms, especially adverbs, which suggest consensus or frequency without necessarily claiming specific proportions or orders of magnitude. Common examples are "typically," "commonly," "widely," "occasionally," "infrequently," or "many." Terms like "majority" which have a specific statistical meaning should be avoided.

Some practitioners argue that it is not necessary to be coy or cautious in one's choice of language since the reader has already been warned that qualitative hypotheses may be modified or rejected in a survey. We believe,

however, that care should be taken to avoid suggesting a statistical frequency since many readers overlook the caveat in making their interpretations and not every qualitative study is followed by a survey. Ambiguity of
any sort is poorly tolerated by most people. Unfortunately, many readers
of qualitative reports resolve the problem by either believing or disbeliev-
ing the statistical reliability of qualitative research.

Should Topic Sentences Be Used?

One common convention of qualitative reports is topic sentences,
used either in place of or in conjunction with section headings and titles.
For example:

- *Consumers fail to distinguish the new skin cleanser concept from ones already
  available.*
- *Physicians are reluctant to expand their responsibility (and their liability) for tests
  now done routinely in private or hospital labs.*

In each case, the italicized statements would be followed by a discussion of
the analyses to support and elaborate on these conclusions.

One advantage of topic sentences over section titles alone (such as
"Image of Premium Beers" or "Product Appeals") is that they summarize
important information at a glance. This act of editorial generosity can be
helpful to both the cursory reader and the thorough one. Equally important, the intellectual discipline required to identify and condense key points
ultimately helps the author interpret and organize the data.

How to Signal Points of Interpretations

Although almost everything written in a qualitative report ultimately
reflects the analytic interpretation of the author, writers frequently need to
distinguish between descriptions of respondents' reactions or opinions and
hypotheses that are meant to explain or account for those reactions. It is
one thing for example, to observe that "respondents vehemently reject
translucent plastic bottles because they are cloudy in color." It is another to
hypothesize that respondents may be acting on the impression that the
contents are somehow contaminated or unclean rather than merely con-
cealed. Statements which require substantial inference on the part of the
author or analyst should be properly flagged, giving the reader an opportunity to test or reject hypotheses which flow from experience and from
insights outside the group discussion.

How Many Quotations?

Qualitative reports commonly contain quotations from respondents
designed to support or illustrate points being made, and if properly se-

lected, these quotes tend to strengthen and enliven a report. How many quotes to use depends on the objectives being served. Where an important goal of the study is to acquaint readers with consumer language, then well-chosen quotes placed liberally throughout the report will certainly help serve that goal.

It is wise, however, to spare the reader tedious excursions through long verbatims for one small interesting tidbit, or through several "irresist-able" quotes to support one small idea. Only important points and particu-larly interesting or pithy quotes deserve inclusion. Quotes which simply restate the point made by the author in just those words or which provide reactions without reason ("I don't know, I just like it") are to be avoided, since they contribute nothing but length to the report.

When selecting quotes, it is important to bear in mind that their purpose is not to prove points but merely to illustrate them. Indeed, while quotes lend face validity to the analysis, the author should not feel obli-gated to support every assertion or conclusion with verbatim accounts. Actually, not every point can be supported with a succinct quote since qualitative analysis by its nature distills and integrates the meaning of many individual statements. Report writers should be guided in making these decisions by the importance of the issue and the availability of relevant statements that genuinely contribute to the reader's understanding.

Individual Depth Interviews

Chapter 18

JUSTIFICATIONS, BENEFITS, AND LIMITATIONS

Although we earlier defined qualitative research as encompassing both individual and group depth interviews, most of this book has been dedicated to group interview methodology. The justification for that emphasis is the complexity and richness of group interviewing. We believe that group depth interview techniques are more difficult to master but are often more productive than individual interviews. While some researchers might take issue with the second point, it is hard to dispute the first. A person who can manage a group interview can conduct an individual interview without further training, but the reverse is not automatically true. Individual interviews are a useful training ground for group moderating skills but do not pose all of the same management challenges.

The relative merit and utility of group interviews over individual interviews is a point on which there is often lively debate. One argument against groups is that they sacrifice some individual depth and detail by tending to preclude a direct response from every participant on every issue. We believe, however, that the benefits of interaction generally tend to outweigh that loss of individual detail. It is not necessary to hear every issue addressed iteratively by every respondent, particularly since an experienced moderator can detect consensus or disagreement on many points by monitoring a group closely. "Equal time per respondent" is far more important when our goal is to tally opinions than it is when we wish to explore their origin and their nature.

It is generally acknowledged that groups tend to represent a more efficient form of data collection than individual depth interviews. A point often overlooked, however, is the extent to which groups afford observers a more interesting and conclusive listening experience than a long series of individual interviews. This is not to suggest that careful tape analysis and reflection are unnecessary; on the contrary, we place great stock in that process. However, observers choose to be present precisely because they seek immediate, even if tentative, feedback, and group data are generally easier to grasp and integrate without benefit of a full analysis than data emerging from perhaps 20 or 30 individual interviews. As a result, observers interpreting individual depth interviews are often tempted to approach the analysis in an additive, almost quantitative fashion and this, of course, violates the spirit of qualitative research.

Individual depth interviews do, however, have a significant role to play in market research. They are, in fact, the qualitative method of choice under certain specific circumstances and deserve at least passing consideration under others.

When Logistical Problems Make Groups Impractical

It may not be feasible or cost efficient to convene group sessions when there is a relatively small pool of eligible candidates from which to choose. Experience suggests that it is difficult to draw a full group with as few 30 eligibles in a single location, although interesting topics, high incentives and extremely energetic recruiting have been known to overcome the odds. If, however, there is less than a quorum in any particular city (certainly fewer than 12), either a mini-group or several individual interviews should be considered. The exceptions are opinion leader groups recruited at sizeable expense from around the country or even around the world. In those cases, the benefits of convening a group of far-flung and preeminent or creative colleagues compensates for the expense and planning requirements of a single session.

When Confidentiality or Antitrust Restrictions Rule Out a Group

It is generally impossible and potentially unlawful to convene a group of CEOs or other senior management representatives from within the same industry, since such a group (even if it could be organized) might convey the appearance of a price collusion. However, confidentiality per se is often a less serious barrier to assembling groups of smaller competitors in the same community. Reticence on some points (for example, gross dollar volume) may be expected in the presence of competitors, but there is never any assurance of complete candor on such issues even in a more private setting. In fact, the presence of knowledgeable competitors in a group interview has been known to prompt greater candor, since individuals who misrepresent themselves or dissemble are gently taken to task.

Moreover, here as with consumers and noncompetitors, interaction can stimulate not only greater candor, but greater self-awareness as well. When a contractor, for example, confessed that even major product improvements by one of his leadng suppliers would not actually prompt him to abandon all his other suppliers, that "surprising" disclosure prompted the rest of the group to review their comments and conclude that they would probably behave in much the same way, lest they lose the "protection" of multiple suppliers. The issue was a critical one for the client: He had been hearing product complaints from his customers, but was reluctant to make costly changes unless substantial volume increases could be expected. As it turned out, his reluctance was well founded.

When the Subject Matter Appears Too Intimate or Sensitive for Group Discussion

Researchers commonly look to individual interviews when the subject matter seems to broach on private or sensitive domains of feelings which they suspect will not be readily or candidly shared in a more public setting. Products relating to personal hygiene needs such as deodorant or mouthwash, or issues like fertility and contraception are often believed to discourage forthright and comfortable discussion.

While subjects like these should at least prompt some consideration of individual interviews, our experience suggests that sensitivity and inhibition are seldom the problem they might seem to be in these areas. In fact, we almost invariably find that groups seem to promote, rather than inhibit, open responses for precisely the same reasons that they seem to stimulate candor on less sensitive topics.

If a group discussion is well moderated by a supportive and nonjudgmental individual, it affords respondents a certain liberty which individual interviews do not in much the way that Alcoholics Anonymous and Weight Watchers draw "confessions" which might not be made in a more intimate setting. In a group of nine or ten, there is always the possibility that one or two courageous individuals will offer information that others would normally prefer to withhold, and thus will tend to provoke private disclosures from the more timid or reticent members.

By contrast, individual interviews can make those disclosures more painful precisely because the isolated respondent has none of the comfort and social support of others being questioned. An interviewer asking questions about oral hygiene, for example, can seem even more formidable or more forward when close physical proximity heightens (rather than diminishes) respondent anxiety about such personal issues as breath or body odor. In a group interview concerning hair loss in women, the presence of peers who shared an embarrassing problem took the edge out of personal disclosures that would have been more painful in a private exchange between a balding respondent and an interviewer with a full head of hair. Similarly, the "we" atmosphere in a group interview with insulin-dependent diabetics helped alleviate the hostility of several young women whose initial response to the interviewer bordered on hostility at being asked to share problems with a healthy nondiabetic.

These arguments are not merely theoretical ones. It has been our repeated experience that respondents can be persuaded to talk in groups about the most intimate matters, including even such delicate subjects as venereal disease. Those who refuse to consider groups for topics like these are overlooking an important principle of group behavior: Revelations love company. If the researcher is genuinely concerned that a subject is too intimate for a group, he or she has equal reason to worry whether the data can be obtained in a more private setting.

When a Case Study Analysis Requires Sustained Individual Focus

Occasionally, researchers wish to develop models of decision making and behavior that are best developed through intensive individual interviews. It may be necessary to converse individually in order to trace a pattern of behaviors without ever losing the train of decision making from beginning to end, or to review records privately with respondents.

In addition, if one wishes to learn how readily individuals can master complex equipment and what engineering adaptations may be necessary to make instruments user friendly, individual interviews are almost always the method of choice. Cases like these are certainly the exception rather than rule in marketing research, however. Those who seek profound psychological insights should not automatically assume that individual interviews are better able to uncover them.

INDIVIDUAL INTERVIEWING TECHNIQUES

The same general principles for posing questions in group depth interviews apply in a one-on-one setting: Be nondirective, be nonjudgmental, and be alert for opportunities to probe. Would-be practitioners, however, should be aware of at least one special handicap they may face in collecting information from an individual respondent without the presence of others to "take the heat off" in a one-on-one interview. The individual depth interviewer must be careful in structuring sustained probes and must recognize when further questioning may actually jeopardize the interview. A respondent may feel hounded, particularly if the interviewer is probing areas that are closely guarded or uncomfortable.

In general, people do not expect to be questioned intensively about their feelings and motivations and they are frequently surprised at the degree of interest a moderator or interviewer will express in ideas they view as inconsequential. They are equally unaccustomed to being pressed to clarify answers they personally view as entirely clear, or obvious; a request to reconsider or reword those responses may thus be viewed as both taxing and threatening. This is not unique to individual interviews but in a group setting, respondents learn what may be expected of them by watching and listening to other exchanges, and they can be rescued from relentless questioning by the interjections of others. When individual probes prove unsuccessful or threatening in a group interview, the moderator can move onto other respondents without losing all the momentum already gained on a particular topic. In a one-on-one situation, the interviewer may have no choice but to back off, at least temporarily, and pursue a fresh avenue of inquiry.

Even while observing the bounds of individual privacy, the interviewers must be careful to convey complete confidence in their right to pose questions. We noted earlier that group interviews actually encourage candor, partly because there are usually some participants who are more prepared than others to offer (and to legitimate) sensitive disclosures early on. In an individual interview, uneasy respondents have no outgoing or garrulous members to emulate. If the interviewer betrays any discomfort with the subject, it is easily detected and tends to close up many relevant avenues of inquiry. There is a general rule of thumb in interviewing of any kind that if the interviewer seems uncomfortable posing a question, the respondent will assume it probably should not be answered. Paradoxically, this problem may be most pertinent in situations where the researcher has chosen individual interviews precisely because the subject matter was believed too sensitive for groups.

Index